AF905038

Social Security Law in the Netherlands

Social Security Law in the Netherlands

Second Edition

Frans Pennings

This book was originally published as a monograph in the International Encyclopaedia of Laws/Social Security Law.

Founding Editor: Roger Blanpain
General Editor: Frank Hendrickx
Volume Editor: Willy van Eeckhoutte

Wolters Kluwer

Published by:
Kluwer Law International B.V.
PO Box 316
2400 AH Alphen aan den Rijn
The Netherlands
Website: www.wolterskluwerlr.com

Sold and distributed in North, Central and South America by:
Wolters Kluwer Legal & Regulatory U.S.
7201 McKinney Circle
Frederick, MD 21704
United States of America
Email: customer.service@wolterskluwer.com

Sold and distributed in all other countries by:
Quadrant
Rockwood House
Haywards Heath
West Sussex
RH16 3DH
United Kingdom
Email: international-customerservice@wolterskluwer.com

DISCLAIMER: The material in this volume is in the nature of general comment only. It is not offered as advice on any particular matter and should not be taken as such. The editor and the contributing authors expressly disclaim all liability to any person with regard to anything done or omitted to be done, and with respect to the consequences of anything done or omitted to be done wholly or partly in reliance upon the whole or any part of the contents of this volume. No reader should act or refrain from acting on the basis of any matter contained in this volume without first obtaining professional advice regarding the particular facts and circumstances at issue. Any and all opinions expressed herein are those of the particular author and are not necessarily those of the editor or publisher of this volume.

Printed on acid-free paper

ISBN 978-90-411-9223-3

e-Book: ISBN 978-90-411-9253-0
web-PDF: ISBN 978-90-411-9287-5

This title is available on www.kluwerlawonline.com

© 2017, Kluwer Law International BV, The Netherlands

All rights reserved. No part of this publication may be reproduced, stored in a retrieval system, or transmitted in any form or by any means, electronic, mechanical, photocopying, recording, or otherwise, without the prior written permission of the publisher.

Permission to use this content must be obtained from the copyright owner. Please apply to: Permissions Department, Wolters Kluwer Legal & Regulatory U.S., 76 Ninth Avenue, 7th Floor, New York, NY 10011-5201, USA. Website: www.wolterskluwerlr.com

Printed and Bound by CPI Group (UK) Ltd, Croydon, CR0 4YY.

The Author

Frans Pennings is a professor in Labour Law and Social Security Law at Utrecht University, the Netherlands. He is also a visiting professor at Gothenburg University, Sweden.
His main research interests are in the areas of national and international social security law and also at the interface between labour law and social security law. In recent years, he has carried out research on the impact of International Labour Organization (ILO) conventions on national systems, on European Union (EU) social security instruments (including Regulation 883/2004) and on Dutch social security law (unemployment, disability and sickness benefits).
He completed comparative studies of the impact of ILO conventions and books on Dutch social security law and labour law in an international context. He is the author and/or editor of nearly forty books and has written more than one hundred articles, book chapters and research reports. His personal website is www.franspennings.org

The Author

Table of Contents

Table of Contents

Table of Contents

Table of Contents

List of Abbreviations

AAW	*Algemene Arbeidsongeschiktheidswet* (General Law Relating to Incapacity for Work)
AB	Administratiefrechtelijke beslissingen
ABW	Algemene Bijstandswet (Public Assistance Law)
AKW	Algemene Kinderbijslagwet (General Child Benefits Law)
AMvB	Algemene Maatregelen van Bestuur
Anw	Algemene Nabestaandenwet (General Survivors Benefits Law)
AOW	Algemene Ouderdomswet (General Old-Age Pension Law)
Arbo	Arbeidsomstandighedenwet (Law on Conditions at the Workplace)
ATW	Arbeidstijdenwet (Working Hours Act)
Awb	Algemene wet bestuursrecht (General Act on Administrative Law)
AWBZ	Algemene Wet Bijzondere Ziektekosten (Law on General Insurance against Special Medical Expenses)
AWW	Algemene Weduwen- en Wezenwet (General Widows' and Orphans' Benefits Act)
BBA	Buitengewoon Besluit Arbeidsverhoudingen (Exceptional Decree on Labour Relations)
BW	Burgerlijk Wetboek (Civil Code)
CBBS	Claim Beoordelings- en Borgingssysteem (Claim Assessment and Control System)
CIZ	Centraal indicatieorgaan zorg (Central Assessment Organisation for Care)
CRvB	Centrale Raad van Beroep (Central Appeals Court)
CVZ	College voor Zorgverzekeringen (Health Care Insurance Board)
CWI	Centra voor werk en inkomen (Centres for Work and Income)
EC	European Commission
ECHR	European Convention on Human Rights
ECR	European Court Reports
EEA	European Economic Area
ESC	European Social Charter
GP	General Practitioner

ILO	International Labour Organization
IOAW	Wet Inkomensvoorziening Oudere en Gedeeltelijk Arbeidsongeschikte Werknemers (Law on Income for Older and Partially Incapacitated Unemployed Persons)
IOAZ	Wet Inkomensvoorziening voor Oudere en gedeeltelijk Arbeidsongeschikte zelfstandigen (Law on Income for Older and Partially Incapacitated Self-Employed)
IVA	*Inkomensvoorziening volledig arbeidsongeschikten* (Income Provision for the Fully Disabled)
IWI	Inspectie Werk en Inkomen (Inspection Work and Income)
RSV	Rechtspraak Sociale Verzekering (Dutch magazine with law reports)
Stb.	Staatsblad (Netherlands Official Journal)
SVB	Sociale Verzekeringsbank (Social Insurance Bank)
TFEU	Treaty on the Functioning of the European Union
Trb.	Tractatenblad (Official Journal of Treaties)
TW	Toeslagenwet (Supplements Act)
Uwv	Uitvoeringsinstituut werknemersverzekeringen (Administration of Employees Insurance Schemes)
VAR	*Verklaring arbeidsrelatie* (Declaration on the Work Relationship)
Wajong	*Wet werk en arbeidsondersteuning jonggehandicapten* (Work and Work Support (Young Disabled Persons) Act)
WAO	Wet op de Arbeidsongeschiktheidsverzekeringen (Law Relating to Insurance against Incapacity for Work)
WAZ	Wet arbeidsongeschiktheidsverzekering zelfstandigen (Invalidity Insurance (Self-Employed Persons) Act)
Wet FSV	Wet Financiering sociale verzekeringen (Act on Financing of Social Insurance Schemes)
Wet Suwi	Wet structuur uitvoeringsorganisatie werk en inkomen (Work and Income Implementation Structure Act)
WGA	Werkhervattingsregeling gedeeltelijk arbeidsgeschikten (Scheme on the Take-Up of Work by Persons Who Are Partially Able to Work)
WIA	Wet werk en inkomen naar arbeidsvermogen (Act on Work and Income According to Working Capacity)
Wlz	Wet Langdurige Zorg (Longterm Care Act)
WMO	Wet Maatschappelijke Ondersteuning (Social Support Act)
WW	Werkloosheidswet (Unemployment Benefits Act)
Wwb	Wet werk en bijstand (Act on Work and Assistance)
Zfw	Ziekenfondswet (Health Insurance Act)

List of Abbreviations

Zvw	Zorgverzekeringswet (Health Insurance Act)
ZW	Ziektewet (Sickness Benefits Act)

General Introduction

§1. General Background

1. The Dutch social security system consists of a number of social insurance schemes on the one hand, and social provisions for specific groups and a general regulation for assistance on the other. The various types of social insurance are outlined in Table 1.

Table 1 Insured Risk

Social Insurance Schemes	*National Insurance Schemes*	*Employees Insurance Schemes*
Sickness		Employers are obliged to pay wages (307 et seq.) Sickness Benefits Act (320 et seq.)
Long-term disability		Disability Insurance Act
Old age	General Old-Age Pension Act (615 et seq.)	
Survivors	General Survivors Act (637 et seq.)	
Children	General Child Benefit Act (264 et seq.)	
Medical	Health Care Insurance Act on Long-term Care (225 et seq.)	
Unemployment		Unemployment Benefits Act (523 et seq.)

2. In addition to the national insurance schemes and the insurance schemes for employees, the social security system consists of social provisions. Some social provisions are meant for specific categories. Examples are: the *Wet Arbeidsongeschiktheidsvoorziening Jonggehandicapten* (Wajong [Young Disabled Persons]) Act) (paragraphs 349 et seq.); the *Toeslagenwet* (TW [Supplements Act]) (paragraphs 545 et seq.); the *Wet Inkomensvoorziening oudere en gedeeltelijk arbeidsongeschikte werknemers* (IOAW [Law on the Income for Older and Partially Incapacitated Unemployed Persons]) (paragraphs 555 et seq.); and *Wet inkomensvoorziening voor oudere en gedeeltelijk arbeidsongeschikte zelfstandigen* (IOAZ [Law on the Income for Older and Partially Incapacitated Self-Employed Persons]) (paragraphs 574 et seq.). Other social provisions are found in the *Wet Maatschappelijke ondersteuning* (WMO [Law on Support by Society]) for, among other things, transport facilities for the disabled (paragraphs 529 et seq.).

3. The *Participatiewet* (Participation Act) (paragraphs 583 et seq.) completes the social security system. This Act provides benefits to any citizen legally residing in the Netherlands who is or is in danger of getting into circumstances in which he does not have the means to provide for the necessary cost of living. This Act provides that a person must first claim any other insurance benefits or special social provisions that he is entitled to before he is entitled to benefit under this Act. If he is then still unable to cover the necessary costs, he may receive a benefit under this Act.

4. In addition to the national insurance and employees' insurance schemes, there are a number of provisions for special groups for which there are separate regulations. These include compensation for the victims of the Second World War, students, persons who are unable to pay the rent due to a low income, visual artists, former inland shipping entrepreneurs and persons living in homes for the elderly. These specific regulations will not be discussed in this volume.

§2. Historical Background

5. One of the earliest Dutch statutory social provisions was the *Armenwet* (Poor Law) of 1818. This Act contained little more than provisions which municipality the poor might turn to for support. Following a change in the Constitution in 1848, a bill for a new *Armenwet* was submitted in 1851, which proposed to give the responsibility for poor relief to the Minister of Home Affairs. The Minister could also set regulations for churches and private charity organizations. However, Parliament rejected the proposal to give public authorities the power over church and private organizations, so a new bill had to be made. This led to the *Armenwet* of 1854 that laid down the principle that poor relief is the responsibility of the church and private organizations. Municipalities were only allowed to help the poor if this was completely unavoidable and after it had been established that no assistance was given by or expected from private organizations.

6. Industrialization came to the Netherlands in the last quarter of the nineteenth century and one of its effects was that an increasing proportion of the labour force became dependent for an income upon employment as an employee. Working conditions at the time were very bad, and the production process in factories led to many casualties. Moreover, in periods of economic decline many people became unemployed. Poor relief often proved to be inadequate for an income.

Soon it became clear that workers needed better protection against new risks such as unemployment and work accidents, and also against older risks including reaching old age. Previous forms of protection (such as support by the family) had lost much of their effectiveness now that workers had moved from rural areas to the cities. Wages were so low that persons were unable to take care of themselves.

These developments required government intervention in order to meet the most urgent needs. Insurance had been hardly developed at this time; the only insurance scheme that existed was for doctor's fees. Some larger firms had schemes for employees or their survivors in case of a calamity, but such schemes were entirely left to the employer's initiative.

7. Industrial accidents occurred frequently and the need for better protection against their consequences was urgent. At the time, the only possibility for getting compensation in case of an industrial accident was to sue the employer under tort law; for this purpose the worker had to satisfy the requirements of tort law, which included proving that the accident was the employer's fault or the result of negligence. This burden of proof was often too heavy for workers, who could not afford legal representation. Workers were often almost illiterate and could not rely on their colleagues to testify in their case, as the colleagues were also dependent on the employer.

The best solution was, therefore, for the State to make a statutory accident insurance law, which relieved employers from liability for compensation in individual cases, and which made it easier for workers to obtain compensation.

8. An important obstacle for the establishment and further development of a statutory social security system was that all the political parties at the time were of the view that the power of the State should remain limited. This was not only the view of the Liberals but also of the Christian parties at the time, which were developing their own communities and wished to protect these from State interference. By introducing compulsory social insurance and compulsory contributions, the State would restrict individual liberties. This attitude against government interference led to a typical Dutch element in the discussions, without foreign counterpart: a so-called legal basis was required for developing a particular statutory social security scheme. By this it was meant that a particular reason to justify government interference was needed.

9. For the first social security system, the *Ongevallenwet* (Industrial Accidents Act), which meant to compensate employees in case of industrial accidents, the legal basis chosen was the so-called *risque professionnel*. By this term it was meant that industrial accidents were part of the risks caused by the production process. Since accidents were an unavoidable part of the industrial process, a social insurance scheme was necessary in order to compensate for the consequences. From this legal basis it followed that only the employers were responsible for the payment of contributions. After several other proposals and discussions, the bill for the *Ongevallenwet* was accepted and the Act came into force in 1901. Initially, the scope of this Act was limited: only employees in dangerous industries specified in the law were covered. In the course of time the law was extended to all employees.

10. Under the *Ongevallenwet*, workers in dangerous industries who earned less than an income as specified in the Act were compulsorily insured. The so-called *Rijksverzekeringsbank* (State Insurance Bank), which had been specially created for administering this Act, laid down the contributions which employers had to pay, based on figures indicating the level of risk. This organization had to be informed if an accident occurred. It would then make enquiries into what benefits the victim or his survivors were entitled to. The benefit available included cash benefits, medical care for the victim and, in case of death, funeral expenses and a pension for the widow and orphans. A separate insurance scheme was made a few years later for sailors and agricultural workers. In 1903 the Mines Act introduced insurance for miners.

11. Discussions on the legal basis revived when a bill for the *Ziektewet* (ZW [Sickness Benefit Act]) was introduced. For this Act, the theory of the deferred wage was mentioned as a legal basis, by which was meant that wages do not only serve to remunerate the present activities of an employee but also guarantee an income during later periods when the employee will not be able to work. It was thought to be unjustified that the employee would have to rely on the Poor Law in periods of inactivity. As workers were rarely in the position to insure themselves, most often they would not have the money for this compulsory insurance, which was deemed necessary to ensure that if a worker was in need he[1] would receive an income 'from his wage'. An implication of the legal basis of the deferred wage was that it was not possible to include the self-employed in the insurance scheme, despite the fact that important groups of the self-employed (such as farmers) often lived in poverty as well.

12. Although the ZW was enacted in 1913, it did not come into force until 1930. This delay was due to a long-lasting debate on the administration of this law. The Government proposed that the State should administer the law, but the political parties in Parliament, referring to the legal basis underlying this Act, argued that from the theory of the deferred wages it followed that the funds should be administered by employers' and employees' representatives. In the discussion in Parliament, the example of the German *Berufsgenossenschaften* was invoked. In this system, organizations of employers having the same type of enterprise were organized to administer the social insurance schemes. This approach won at the expense of the system proposed by the Government, where the State was to administer the benefits. So-called *bedrijfsverenigingen*, associations governed by employers' and employees' organizations were created to administer the employees' insurance scheme. These organizations remained to exist until 1997 and were then replaced by what is now the *Uitvoeringsinstuut werknemersverzekeringen* (Uwv [Administration of Employees Insurance Schemes]).

13. Under the ZW, workers who earned less than the income level stipulated in this Act were insured against the financial consequences of being incapacitated as a result of illness of invalidity. This was also true for the *Invaliditeitswet* (Invalidity Benefit Act), which was also adopted in this period. At the time, reaching old age was considered to be a form of invalidity and covered by this act. In case of the insured person's decease, his survivors received a pension.

14. The cost of medical care was not included in these insurance schemes. The reason for this was that doctors preferred to leave the medical expenses insurance scheme with the existing organizations, i.e., the health insurance funds, and the legislator concurred with this.

15. A provision was made in the Sickness Benefit Act that payment of sickness benefits could be refused if a worker had not insured himself with a health insurance fund. Compulsory insurance against medical expenses was not introduced until 1941.

1. Where the pronoun 'he' or 'his' is used, the reader is asked to read, where relevant, also 'she' or 'her'.

16. The *Kinderbijslagwet voor loontrekkenden* (Family Allowance Act for Wage Earners) came into force in 1939. On the basis of this Act, workers who had more than two children were entitled to child benefit.

17. A statutory unemployment insurance scheme was not adopted before 1949. Although the British *National Insurance Act* of 1911 and the German *Gesetz über Arbeitsvermittlung und Arbeitslosenversicherung* (1927) were known in the Netherlands, these examples were not a reason to adopt also unemployment insurance in the Netherlands because of the high unemployment levels in the 1930s. Until the Act came into force, the unemployed had to rely on funds created by trade unions and municipalities which were subsided on the basis of circulars or laws by the State. From trade union funds payments were made to trade union members who had become unemployed. More and more local authorities had started to support these union funds with subsidies. During the 1914–1918 World War, when the rate of unemployment rose sharply, the State also decided to grant subsidies. Foreign examples from Ghent and from Denmark were relevant to the subsidy method. In the Ghent model, the municipal government increased the benefits paid by the trade union by a certain percentage. In the Danish model, the subsidy was related to the contributions paid by the insured to the fund. The Netherlands chose the Danish model in the *Werkloosheidsbesluit* (1917) and the *Werkloosheidsverzekeringsnoodwet* (1919), two unemployment schemes.[2] Unemployment benefits were payable for a maximum of thirteen weeks. After that period, unemployed person became dependent on municipal poor relief provisions as regulated in the already mentioned *Armenwet* of 1912 (Poor Law). Like its predecessor, the *Armenwet* of 1854, this Act required that claimants relied on the help of family, church and private charity organizations first. Only in cases where help was unavailable or insufficient would local authorities guarantee essential living expenses. The 1912 *Armenwet* made the municipality responsible for proper medical care by local doctors and midwives for the poor.

18. During the Second World War, the Dutch Government was in exile in London where, in 1942, the *Beveridge Report* was published.[3] This report was a blueprint for the future of British social security. Inspired by the Beveridge Report, the Dutch government established the so-called Commission Van Rhijn which had to sketch the foundations of the future Dutch social security system. Its report was published as *Sociale Zekerheid* (Social Security).[4] The report starts with a description of the development of social insurance during the War in several countries, in particular in the allied countries. On the basis of this, it proposed a new legal basis, that was to become very important for the development of Dutch social security. The new legal basis read that the Community, organized in the State, is responsible for the social security and the protection against poverty of all its members, on condition that these members do all they can reasonably do to provide for their own protection against poverty through their own efforts. This legal basis was accepted by the Government

2. See on the funds, F. Pennings, *Benefits of Doubt: A Comparative Study of the Legal Aspects of Employment and Unemployment Schemes in Great Britain, Germany, France and the Netherlands* 300 (Kluwer Law International 1990).
3. W. Beveridge, *Social Security and Allied Services*, Cmnd. 6404 (HMSO 1942).
4. *Sociale Zekerheid* (*Social Security*) (Staatsuitgeverij 1945).

and made it possible to extend the scope of the social security system beyond the category of employees.

19. The responsibility of the State for the whole population led to the introduction of insurance schemes covering all residents, i.e., national insurance schemes. The first of these schemes was the *Algemene Ouderdomswet* (AOW [General Old-Age Pensions Law]), which came into force on 1 January 1957. This law provides for flat rate non-means tested-benefits, the level of which depends on the type of household. The Dutch schemes differ in several respects from their British equivalents. Unlike the British Social Security Act, which covers all risks, separate Acts were made for each risk in the Dutch system. Moreover, unlike British social security, the Dutch national insurance schemes are not administered by the State but by a newly created benefit administration, later to be called the *Sociale Verzekeringsbank* (SVB [Social Insurance Bank]).

20. The national insurance schemes were added to the existing system of employees' insurance schemes. It was by no means intended that from then on only one type of social security scheme was to exist. Indeed, after the war new employees' insurance schemes were introduced, such as the *Werkloosheidswet* (1949) (WW [Unemployment Benefits Act]). Another employees' insurance scheme was the *Ziekenfondswet* (Zfw [Health Insurance Act]), which covers employees earning a wage below a specified level against medical costs and also, from 2000, self-employed persons with a low income.

The combination of employees' insurance and national insurance schemes made a unique, but also complicated, patchwork quilt, still a main characteristic of Dutch social security.

21. The first social insurance scheme covering the entire population, the AOW, covers all residents and persons not residing, but working in the Netherlands. They are compulsorily insured under this Act. The financial means for paying the pensions and administration costs are obtained from contributions. Contributions are calculated as a percentage of a person's wage or income up to a maximum amount stipulated in the Act. Contributions are collected by the Tax Office and are subsequently transferred to the Old Age Pension Fund, which is managed by the SVB. The old-age pension is flat rate and is subject to reductions if the individual pensioner was not insured at any particular time during the period between ages 15 and 67, or if he has been culpable of negligence with regard to the payment of contributions.

22. A second national insurance scheme was the *Algemene Weduwen- en Wezenwet* (AWW [General Widows' and Orphans' Benefits Law]) which came into force on 1 October 1959. Under this Act, flat-rate benefits were payable to widows and orphans. It was later replaced by the *Algemene Nabestaandenwet.*

23. National insurance schemes for long-term disability, medical expenses and accommodation in institutions for people with long-term illnesses and disabilities took a longer time to develop. This can partly be explained by the fact that all kinds of practical and technical problems had to be resolved first. Moreover, the question to what degree the State has the responsibility of social security for its subjects was discussed at great length. The citizen's individual responsibility and his right to determine to what extent he would like to insure himself against specific risks had to be weighed against the State's responsibility for the welfare of all its subjects. Eventually this resulted in two more social security Acts: the *Algemene Arbeidsongeschiktheidswet*

(AAW [General Law Relating to Incapacity for Work]) and the *Algemene Wet Bijzondere Ziektekosten* (AWBZ [Law on General Insurance against Special Medical Expenses]), which were adopted in the 1960s. The former Act was repealed in the 1990s, and the latter was replaced by the *Wet Langdurige Zorg* (Wlz) in 2015.

24. The employees' insurance system that had been established before the Second World War was thoroughly changed in 1967. A new Act was introduced for benefits for the disabled, the *Wet op de Wet op de Arbeidsongeschiktheidsverzekeringen* (WAO [Law Relating to Insurance against Incapacity for Work]). The WAO replaced the pre-war disability Acts, the *Ongevallenwet* and the *Invaliditeitswet*. An important characteristic of the WAO was that the cause of incapacity for work became irrelevant for purposes of benefit eligibility. Consequently, there was no longer any distinction between occupational accidents or diseases (previously insured by the *Ongevallenwet*) and general accidents and diseases (previously insured by the *Invaliditeitswet*). The WAO provided for a wage-related benefit to disabled employees after they were incapacitated for work for a period of fifty-two weeks (during the first year of incapacity for work, the Sickness Benefits Act (ZW) guaranteed the entitlement to sickness benefits for insured employees). There was no requirement on the duration of insured periods which determines eligibility for benefit. The amount of benefit was related to the loss of earnings capacity of the claimant. In addition, the WAO contained provisions for the maintenance, restoration or promotion of capacity to work.

25. This system of employee insurance schemes acted as a model for the national insurance for the disabled, the AAW, which came into operation in 1975 and existed alongside with the WAO. The AAW entitled all residents from age 18 up to the age of 65 to benefit in case of full or partial disability. The actual benefit was a percentage of a rate that was related to the subsistence minimum (the same as the net minimum wage); the percentage depended on the level of disability. The provisions relating to the maintenance, restoration and promotion of a person's capacity to work were no longer made by virtue of the WAO but were now included in the AAW. For those entitled to WAO benefit, the AAW benefit was fully deducted from their benefit.

26. The abolition of accident insurance legislation resulted in the provisions in those Acts concerning medical treatment and care being transferred, in 1967, to the health insurance scheme for employees regulated in the Zfw and to the Wlz.

27. The end of the economic growth which came in the early 1970s led to changes in the social security system and to separate Acts. Drastic measures were taken both in the areas of financing and of organizing the system, benefit administration and benefit levels. Benefit levels were reduced; benefit duration was shortened, and the conditions for entitlement were tightened. In the 1990s and in the beginning of the twenty-first century, there were more radical changes to the principles of the system. These will be discussed in the sections to come, but here we can already mention some major changes. These changes put a strong emphasis on activation, i.e., the responsibility of benefit claimants, but also their counterparts, such as employers, to keep benefit claims as small as possible.

28. For the ZW this meant that as of 1996, the role of this Act was reduced; instead under the provisions of the *Burgerlijk Wetboek* (BW [Civil Code]) the employer is obliged to continue to pay wages to his ill employees; initially this was for a maximum period of six weeks, later this was extended to fifty-two weeks, and as of 2005 the maximum period is even 104 weeks. The ZW now serves as a safety net only, i.e., if for persons who do not have an employer anymore and not specified categories of persons. This is called the privatization of the ZW.

29. In 1996 the AWW was replaced with the *Algemene Nabestaandenwet* (Anw [General Survivors Benefits Act]), which provides for benefit under much more restricted conditions than its predecessor. A major change was the introduction of a means test in the new Act.

30. For persons who became disabled as of 1 January 2006, the *Wet werk en inkomen naar arbeidsvermogen* (WIA [Law on Work and Income According to Work Capacity]) provides for disability benefit; the WAO remains to exist for old cases. The WIA makes a distinction between persons who are permanently fully disabled and others. For these others a distinction in benefit level is made between those who earn a certain level of income and those who cannot; for the former category, the benefit level is higher. The new system was drafted this way in order to encourage employment.

31. A new national insurance was established in 2006 for health care costs, the *Zorgverzekeringswet* (Zvw [Health Insurance Act]). This law is administered by private insurance companies and replaced the Zfw.

32. The *Algemene Bijstandswet* (ABW [Public Assistance Act]), which replaced certain parts of the former Poor Law, was a general safety net. This Act was put into operation in 1965 and it made financial provisions for residents who are unable to meet the basic costs of living. This Act is implemented by the local authorities and financed from general government and municipal financial sources. It was replaced with a new public assistance Act in 1996, and finally, by the *Participatiewet*, which requires particular counteractivities of persons claiming social assistance.

§3. Sources of Social Security Law

I. General

33. The main sources of Dutch social security law are Acts of Parliament and implementation regulations, case law and international treaties. Before we discuss these sources, we shall first look briefly at what the Constitution provides on social security.

II. Legislation

A. Constitution

34. Initially, the only provision on social protection in the Constitution concerned the care of the poor. Article 141 of the 1814 Constitution provided that the government make permanent provision for the care of the poor and the upbringing of poor children. In 1848, the requirement was added that the care of the poor had to be regulated by the Act of Parliament. It was not until 1983 that an article laying down the right to social security and assistance was incorporated into the Constitution, in the chapter on fundamental rights. This article reads:

Article 20 of the Constitution:

(1) The social protection of the population and distribution of welfare are matters of concern for the government.
(2) Rules are laid down in acts of parliament governing entitlement to social security.
(3) Dutch people resident in the Netherlands who are unable to support themselves have a right to receive social assistance from the authorities as regulated by an Act adopted by Parliament.

+

35. The historical survey given above shows that legislation regulating entitlement to social security benefits was made already before this article was included in the Constitution. For the future, it is relevant that when changes to legislation are introduced, the legislator should check whether these changes meet the constitutional requirement of Article 20. Courts cannot test compatibility of statutes with the Constitution; instead they can do so with respect to international treaties (*see* paragraphs 42 ff. below).

B. Statutes

36. Social security law in the Netherlands is mainly laid down in Acts adopted by Parliament. The historical survey given in the previous section shows that social security legislation was not made as a result of a certain plan. Legislation has been developed in the course of history to meet needs arising within society and pressure from various social groups and, at the same time, its development depended on economic resources. When private initiatives were lacking or were insufficient, the legislator interfered, as was the case, for example, in 1901 when the *Ongevallenwet* (Industrial Accidents Act) was passed. On such occasions and conditions, the government could make its own proposals with regard to the contents of the Act and the way of implementation. If, however, there were private regulations, for instance on the basis of collective labour agreements or schemes initiated by employers' organizations or big enterprise or trade unions, the legislator strove to conform to these schemes. In the 1960s, the role of the government became to be not subsidiary anymore, as the State's responsibility became predominant. As from the 1990s, however, the role of the State became more subsidiary, although in a different way as before, since the State now clearly defines the responsibilities of the various actors, such as the obligation of employers to pay wages to their ill employees.

C. Implementing Regulations

37. Social security Acts frequently contain instructions for further rules to be laid down in general legislative measures (called *Algemene Maatregelen van Bestuur* (AMvB)), Royal Decrees or ministerial regulations. Sub-delegation is permitted. The benefit administration is also authorized to make further rules. As a result, social security law has become quite complicated

38. For the actual administration of benefits, internal regulations are also made which make clear how the benefit officers have to Act in specific, frequently occurring cases. These so-called *beleidsregels* (policy rules) do not have the effect of an Act, but they are of important legal value, particularly when they are published, since the benefit administration is expected to work in conformity with these rules. If it does not, it has to give good arguments for not doing so, and if such are lacking the court may quash the benefit administration's decision for not being consistent with the policy rules.

39. In cases where the benefit administration has been given a certain degree of freedom of policy-making, the judge will test this policy only marginally, i.e., he will enquire whether the benefit administration could reasonably have come to the decision as it did under the given circumstances.

D. Adjudication

40. Case law is a major source of law. When a decision is taken, the applicant first has to follow a review procedure before the benefit administration itself, before he can go to court.

41. When the outcome of the review procedure is unfavourable for him, the applicant can go to court, i.e., the *rechtbank* (Court of First Instance). Further appeal is possible to the *Centrale Raad van Beroep* (CRvB [Central Appeals Court]).[5] There are several periodicals which publish the decisions of the courts; these decisions are selected by independent reviewers. Important case law magazines are *Rechtspraak Sociale Verzekering* (RSV), *Uitspraken sociale zekerheid* (USZ) and *Administratiefrechtelijke beslissingen* (AB). Decisions can now also be found on www.rechtspraak.nl. There are very few decisions translated into English.

E. Treaties

42. Articles 93 and 94 of the Constitution provide that treaty provisions and decrees of international organizations that, given their contents, bind all citizens are part of national law; national statutory provisions that are incompatible with these international provisions and decrees cannot be applied. It is up to the national court to decide whether an international provision has such an effect. Also, in social security there are court decisions in which national provisions are not applied because of their incompatibility with international law.[6]

43. The following instruments are of particular importance for social security law:

5. CRvB, *see* www.rechtspraak.nl/Organisatie/CRvB/OverDeCRvB/Pages/English-review.aspx (accessed on 11 Dec. 2016).
6. See Frans Pennings (ed.), *Between Soft and Hard Law: The Impact of International Social Security Standards on National Social Security Law* (Kluwer Law International 2006).

(a) The Treaty on the Functioning of the European Union (TFEU) and the regulations issued on the basis of this treaty, such as Regulation 883/2004 and Regulation 492/2011, as well as the directives based on that treaty (such as Directive 79/7) have greatly influenced Dutch social security law. EU regulations must be applied in the Member States. In case of a conflict between a Dutch Act and an EU regulation, the regulation takes precedence. Directives have to be implemented in the Member States within the stipulated implementation period.
(b) The European Convention for the Protection of Human Rights and Fundamental Freedom (ECHR, 1950) of the Council of Europe.
(c) The International Treaty on Civil and Political Rights, as well as the International Treaty on Economic, Social and Cultural Rights (New York, 1966) established by the United Nations.
(d) Provisions of Conventions adopted by the International Labour Organization (ILO) may have direct effect as well.[7]

7. See previous note, and also Frans Pennings (ed.), *International Social Security Standards: Current Views and Interpretation Matters* (Antwerp 2007), which also contains those Dutch decisions (translated into English).

Part I. The Institutions

Chapter 1. Introduction

44. In this part, we will discuss the main organizations involved in the administration of social security law. These are mostly organizations which exclusively or essentially deal with social security tasks; in addition we will mention shortly public law institutions which are partially involved in social security as part of serving public administration. The final responsibility for the proper administration of social security legislation lies with the Minister of Social Affairs and Employment, who is at all times accountable to Parliament.

The benefit administrations, which are not a part of the public service and which cannot be considered as parts of the regular civil service, but whose obligations are defined by a statutory Act, are at all times obliged to supply information and to account for their decisions to the politically responsible officials in some form or other.

45. The agreements and recommendations of the ILO contain provisions which endorse the desirability of calling in employers' and employees' organizations for the administration of social security legislation. In this way, the involvement of parties who have an interest either as contribution payers or as benefit claimants may be increased. Furthermore, they may contribute to a better adjustment of statutory social security to regulations in the private domain that were made by them. This is of particular importance as nowadays there is an increased need and desire for individual responsibility, with reduced government intervention. The question of whether and how the government can best realize its responsibility to realize the right of individuals to sufficient means of existence, for adequate medical care and other human rights, as stated in the Universal Declaration of Human Rights, must therefore be answered in close consultation with those directly involved. By actively cooperating in the administration of the social security laws, the parties involved can increase their knowledge of the system and its effects and subsequently can participate in these consultations. Consequently, they also will be better equipped to make agreements and regulations in the private domain which will be properly attuned to the statutory regulations.

46. In the Netherlands, in the past decades, social security expenditure on incapacity to work benefits increased at a much more rapid pace than in neighbouring countries; the percentage of people who were incapacitated surpassed those abroad. In order to discover the exact cause of this phenomenon, Parliament launched an official investigation. This brought to light that the benefit administration had adopted a too broad interpretation of disability legislation, in particular where the concepts of illness and incapacity to work were concerned. Furthermore, it became clear that the supervision of the benefit administration was inadequate. This investigation resulted in a radical change of the organization of supervision and administration, as we will discuss below. The role of the social partners in the decision-making of the benefit administrations was radically reduced.

Chapter 2. Old Age, Survivors and Child Benefit Schemes

§1. Administration

47. The old age, survivors and child benefit insurance Acts are national insurance schemes. This means that, in principle, all residents are insured under these Acts.

Insured persons are obliged to pay contributions for the old age and survivors insurance schemes. These contributions are calculated as a percentage of the annual wage or income and are levied by the Tax Office together with income tax. Child benefits are financed from public funds (taxes).

48. The SVB was set up to manage the funds, to carry out the administration of these Acts and to pay the benefits. Chapter 6 of the *Wet structuur uitvoeringsorganisatie werk en inkomen* (Wet Suwi [Work and Income Implementation Structure Act]) gives rules on SVB.

49. The SVB has legal personality and is governed by a board consisting of four members and an advisory council. The decisions are made by the board; the council gives advice to the board. The members of both bodies are appointed and dismissed by the Minister of Social Affairs and Employment.

50. The board of the SVB has to ensure that beneficiaries or their representatives are involved in the decision-making process on the administration of benefits.

51. Article 34 of the Wet Suwi provides that the SVB is charged with the administration of the old-age benefits scheme, the survivors benefits scheme and the child benefit scheme as stipulated by law, insofar as that administration has not been assigned to others by virtue of the law. Since 2002, it is no longer the task of the SVB but rather the task of the municipalities to promote employment opportunities of persons receiving benefits under the Anw. In addition, the bank is charged with the management and administration of the Old Age Benefit Fund, the Survivors Benefit Fund and the General Child Benefit Fund.

§2. Supervision

52. The administration by the SVB is supervised by the *Inspectie Werk en Inkomen* (IWI [Inspection Work and Income]), which is part of the Ministry of Social Affairs and Employment. This Inspectorate also supervises the administration of the disability and unemployment insurance schemes by the Uwv.

53. The inspectorate is charged with the supervision of the legitimacy and efficiency of the administration of Acts by the organizations under its supervision. This task is described in Article 37 of the Wet Suwi.

54. The IWI is responsible for the supervision of public assistance as well.

Chapter 3. Sickness Benefit, Disability and Unemployment and Related Schemes

§1. ADMINISTRATION

55. Chapter 5 of the Wet Suwi deals with the Uwv. The Uwv was introduced in 2002 after a reorganization of the benefit administration organizations. This reorganization was the outcome of years of discussion. After initial plans to privatize the benefit administrations completely (they would have to compete with other providers, such as private insurance companies, to get a contract with the State for administering benefits), the government changed its view completely and decided that benefit administration had to remain a public task, because of the public responsibilities following from *inter alia* the Constitution.

56. The Uwv has a central office with local offices. It administers the ZW, the WAO, the WIA and the WW and the TW.

57. A second element of the reorganization is that payment of benefits and reintegration efforts is more closely linked. This was done by giving Uwv also this task, which is performed by Uwv WERKbedrijf.

58. The Uwv's main task is the administration of employees' insurance schemes. In addition, the Uwv sees to the administration of *Wet Wajong (Wet Voorzieningen Jonggehandicapten* (Young Disabled Persons Act) (and the TW).

59. Other bodies are also involved in the implementation of these Acts, e.g., the Tax Office, which collects the contributions for employees' insurance and national insurance schemes.

60. The Uwv is governed by a board consisting of a chairman and a number of members to be determined by the Minister of Social Affairs and Employment.

§2. SUPERVISION

61. The previously mentioned (paragraphs 51 et seq.) IWI is also charged with the supervision of the administration of disability and unemployment insurance schemes. This supervisory task extends to the Uwv and the administrative bodies and is further described in the Suwi Act. It is practically the same as the supervisory responsibility towards the SVB.

Chapter 4. Medical Insurance Schemes

§1. Administration

62. The Zvw and the Wlz both give care provisions: provisions to prevent illness, medical treatment, cure and care to an extent to be described further. Until 2006, the Zfw was in force, an employees' insurance scheme that protected employees and self-employed persons with low incomes only. The Zvw is a national scheme which covers all residents, regardless of income.

The Zvw is administered by private insurance companies. The basic provisions of the insurance are mentioned in the Zvw, which means that insurance companies are bound by these provisions, but the companies themselves fix the contributions for the insurances they sell. For persons with high costs (special diseases, etc.), there is a common insurance fund to which the employers of the insured persons contribute, as well as those insured persons (e.g., the self-employed) who do not have an employer.

63. The Wlz is a national insurance scheme for all residents from the day they are born until the day they die. The benefits provided by the Zvw and the Wlz are defined in decrees.

The private companies often offer supplementary insurances which supplement the compulsory insurance for provisions not covered by the statutory insurance schemes and which can be bought by persons who have also bought the basis insurance These supplementary insurances are voluntary and completely subject to private law.

64. The private companies also administer the Wlz for those persons who are client for their Zvw insurance.

65. In addition to the above-mentioned organizations, the so-called liaison offices and the Central Administration Office are to be mentioned, which were established on the basis of the Wlz. They take care of the administration and supervision of some of the benefits paid by the implementing bodies.

§2. Supervision

66. The *Nederlandse Zorgautoriteit* (Care Authority) has been entrusted with the general supervision of provisions payable on the basis of the Zvw and Wlz.

67. The *Zorginstituut Nederland* (Care Institute Netherlands) is responsible for advice on the contents of the care to be provided by the Zvw and the Wlz. It advises the Minister on the contents of the decree which defines the provisions payable on the basis of the Zvw (statutory basis insurance) and Wlz.

68. The *Zorginstituut* gives advice in individual cases where there is a dispute on whether a particular treatment is covered by the statutory basis insurance. Courts can decide on these issues only after the advice is given.

69. The *Zorginstituut* redistributes the money of the solidarity fund payable for the cure and care of the so-called risk groups (groups with extraordinary costs) over the Insurance companies which actually have these expenses. Examples are the group of very old persons and in particular the patient groups.

70. The financial means required for the Wlz are also collected in a fund, the General Exceptional Medical Expenses Fund, which is managed by the *Zorginstituut*.

Chapter 5. Social Provisions

71. On the basis of the Constitution, all citizens are entitled to public assistance if they are unable to support themselves if they reside in the Netherlands.

72. The *Participatiewet* provides which bodies are involved in the administration of these regulations. The municipalities are charged with the administration of this Act. Normally, a special municipal department takes care of the administration, under the responsibility of the municipal authorities.

73. The Minister of Social Affairs and Employment supervises the administration of the *Participatiewet* by the municipalities. The financial responsibility of the Act lies completely with the municipalities.

74. The municipalities also administer the IOAW, the IOAZ and the WMO.

Part II. Contribution and Financing

Chapter 1. Introduction

75. Social insurance schemes (national insurance schemes and employees insurance schemes) are mainly financed from contributions made by the parties involved, i.e., the insured persons and, in case of insurance schemes for employed persons, also by the employers.

76. Social provisions are financed by public funds. The larger part of this is financed by the State, but the *Participatiewet* is paid by the municipalities. We will not delve further into the financing of social provisions.

77. Reintegration measures are paid by the benefit administrations and in some cases by employers.

78. Contributions for national insurance schemes and employees insurance schemes are collected by the Tax Office. This office transfers the money collected to the various funds. This subject will be discussed in more detail in Chapter 2.

79. Since 1989 one of the national insurance schemes is no longer paid from taxes, namely the *Algemene Kinderbijslagwet* (AKW [General Child Benefit Insurance Act]). The financial means required for the administration of this Act are fully supplied by the State.

80. The employees insurance schemes are also mainly financed from the contributions. Employers are obliged to pay the contributions (due by them and by the employees) to the Uwv. As mentioned above, the Tax Office is responsible for collecting these contributions.

Chapter 2. Contributions Regulations for Employee Insurance Schemes

81. The employee insurance schemes regulated in the WW, the ZW, the WIA and the WAO are financed from contributions.

82. There is no separate contribution anymore (after the introduction of the obligation of employers to continue to pay wages in case of sickness) for the ZW. The ZW benefits are financed from contributions that are levied for the WW, *see* paragraphs 118 et seq.

83. Persons who are insured and their employers are liable to pay contributions for the WW. The WIA contributions are paid solely by the employers of those who are insured.

§1. Field of Application

I. Territorial Field of Application

84. In principle, the employee insurance schemes cover persons working in the Netherlands; all activities carried out in employment in the Netherlands lead to compulsory insurance. This is also the starting point of Regulation 883/2004. This starting point has been laid down in Article 11 of that regulation. In addition, paragraph 1 of said Article states that a person can only be subject to the legislation of one Member State. This rule for determining the legislation applicable has exclusive effect, which means that it prevents the co-occurrence of the legislation of more than one Member State. It also has an overriding effect in that the system assigned by the rules for determining the applicable legislation applies regardless of the contents of the stipulations in the designated scheme that define the coverage by the statutory insurance in relation to foreign schemes.

85. In the *Besluit uitbreiding en beperking kring werknemersverzekeringen* (Decree on the extension and limitation of the personal scope of employees insurance schemes) gives rules on the extension and limitation of the personal scope, which is comparable to (but not the same as) the decree on national insurance schemes. For example, employees who live in the Netherlands and work abroad and personnel of consular posts of international organizations and of the Dutch Antilles and Aruba who are employed in the Netherlands are excluded.

86. In Article 9, foreigners who are crew members of a sea-going vessel and who are living on board that vessel are excluded from the insurance. Articles 13 and 14 concern persons who live abroad and are only working in the Netherlands for a short period of time (musicians, artists). Finally, Article 15 provides that the benefit administration, the Uwv, has the power to decide, upon request, that an employee be excluded from the insurance, provided that he does not live in the Netherlands on a long-term basis, he is employed by a foreign non-profit organization established in the Netherlands and he is insured on the basis of the social security system of another country. Such a request for exemption from the Dutch insurance scheme may only be made by the organization by which the person in question is employed. The duration of the exemption is two years maximum and can be extended after each request. It is possible to make a request at the end of each two-year period.

II. Personal Field of Application

A. The Definition of Employees

87. The definition of insured persons is almost identical for the WW, the WIA (Disability Insurance Act) as well as the ZW. This group consists mainly of employees.

88. The question of who is considered to be the employer in view of the employee insurance schemes will not be dealt with separately.

89. Insured for the ZW, WIA and WW is an employee, who is a natural person, under the age of 65, and who has a private or public employment relationship. A person works in a private employment relationship when he works for an employer on the basis of a contract of employment. A person works in a public employment relationship when he is employed by a public body. When a person holds a public office after being elected, he is not considered to be in a public or private employment relationship; special social security arrangements apply for this person.

90. As from 2001, all civil servants are within the personal scope of employee insurance schemes.

91. Insurance is compulsory for persons in public and in private employment irrespective of the number of working hours of their contract. The only exception made is in the case of persons who do housekeeping work for a natural person: if, as a rule, this work is done in less than four days per week, the job is not insured for the employees' insurance schemes (*see* paragraph 125).

92. In 1998 an Act came into force which inserted in the ZW, the WW and the WAO a provision that a foreigner is not considered to be an employee if he has not been admitted unconditionally to the Netherlands (in the sense of the Aliens Act). Exceptions to this rule can be made by Royal Decree. This rule now also applies for the WIA, the successor of the WAO.

93. A contract of employment is deemed to exist when all the requirements of Article 7:610 of the BW are met. These are the following: the employee must be committed to do the work himself (so he cannot ask someone else to do the work); the employer must be obliged to pay wages; the employee has to be subject to the instructions of the employer; and the work has to be done 'during a certain period of time'. In the next paragraphs, we will deal with the various elements of the contract of employment in more detail.

94. The employee has to perform work. The concept of work should be interpreted in the broadest sense. It includes both physical and mental work; attendance duties are also considered as work.[8] The work has to be done by the employee himself; if the work may be delegated to someone else, there is no contract of employment in most

8. HR 15 Mar. 1991, *NJ* 1991, 417.

cases. A further condition is that the employer has to pay a remuneration for the work (wages).

95. A very important condition is that the employee has to be subject to the powers of the employer to give him instructions. This means that he has to carry out his employer's instructions and orders. In fact, this is the most important criterion, but also the criterion which is the most difficult to check. It regularly leads to problems, particularly in situations in which the employee has been given a considerable degree of freedom to do his work. Positions such as that of a physician, a sales representative, a researcher or a legal advisor are very often practised as independent professions. They may, however, also be performed on the basis of a contract of employment. In such cases, a further investigation of the facts may be required in order to come to a decision.

96. In some cases, even persons working on the basis of a contract of employment are not considered employed persons for the employees insurance schemes, as the Central Appeals Court decided that they were not subordinated to an employer. This is the case of a person who possesses the majority of shares of the company by which he is employed and therefore in effect has control of the company.[9] This decision was made because the Court considered that it would be unjustified when a person was in a position to influence his benefit position; for instance, a main shareholder can first give himself a high wage and then dismiss himself and claim high unemployment benefit. Since 1 January 1998, this case law is laid down in the Acts on the employees' insurance schemes (paragraph 125) and the main shareholder is now excluded from coverage by employees insurance schemes.[10]

97. There may also be doubts in other situations whether a person works in subordination to an employer, an example being flex work. In these work relations, the question arises not only whether there is a contract of employment, but also for how many hours. In order to make it easier to answer these questions, a provision was inserted into the Civil Code stating that a person who has worked during three consecutive months, every week or at least twenty hours per month, for another person for a remuneration paid by that other person is presumed to do this work on the basis of a contract of employment.

In 2001, there was another change in the law which made it easier to define who is an employee and who is self-employed. This is the so-called declaration of self-employment, issued on request by the Tax Office. This declaration was meant to give more certainty to persons who claim to be self-employed and their contract parties. This declaration was, in principle, binding for the Uwv. The *Verklaring arbeidsrelatie* (VAR [Declaration on the Work Relationship]) was a document issued by the Tax Office stating the type of work relationship. This was relevant for the contract partner, as he could now be certain that he did not have to deduct employees contributions from the remuneration. However, it appeared that the declarations were issued in many cases where a person was not really self-employed, because it appeared hard to distinguish self-employed and employees. Therefore in 2016 a new Act came into force, the *Wet deregulering arbeidsrelaties* (Act on the deregulation of employment relationships). However, this act was applied so strictly, that many applications were

9. CRvB 4 Oct. 1985, RSV 1986, 21.
10. See for instance, HR 7 Feb. 1940, *NJ* 1940, 180.

rejected. The application of the Act is now suspended until 2018, and the more generous treatment of self-employed seems to be applied again. The issue of the distinction between employed and self-employed persons is a hot topic in the Netherlands; it does not concern only the distinction between self-employed and employed persons, but also the discussion to what extent there should be difference in coverage of these groups.

98. The fourth element of the contract of employment is that the labour relationship is entered into 'for a certain period of time'. The meaning of this requirement is debatable. Several authors claim that it has no decisive meaning. It may be used, however, to exclude very marginal jobs, such as reading electricity meters in the last month of the year by students or by collecting strawberries during the summer holidays by children.

99. Sometimes the law explicitly provides that certain activities are carried out on the basis of a contract of employment. In this respect, attention should be paid to the fact that since 1999 all work done for an agency for temporary work is done on the basis of a contract of employment (Article 7:690 Civil Code). Consequently, temporary workers are covered by the statutory employee insurance schemes on the ground that they have a contract of employment.

B. Extension of the Concept of Employed Person

100. Over the years, the group of persons covered by employee insurance schemes has been extended to groups of persons whose work relationships are not based on contracts of employment but on a different kind of agreement or contract (*see* below, paragraphs 120 et seq.). Tax legislation has seen a similar development upon the introduction of the Tax on Wages Act of 1964. According to that Act, the employer is obliged to deduct the tax on wages due by the employee from his wages. The employer would have difficulties in doing this if the concepts of 'employee' and 'wages' were not highly assimilated for the social insurance and tax legislation. Articles 3 and 4 of the Tax on Wages Act of 1964 are practically identical to Articles 4 and 5 of the employee insurance Acts.

101. In Article 4 of the employee insurance Acts, the legislator (in addition to the definition of employed person in Article 3 of these Acts) has put a number of work relationships on a par with employed persons. Article 5 gives the powers to assimilate also several other types of work relationships with employees by general legislative measure.

Article 4 of the employee insurance Acts describes various types of work relationships that, under certain conditions, are put on a par with employment. This concerns, for instance, small-scale contractors and their assistants who, not as self-employed, himself performs a work. Commercial agents, fishermen, apprentices and board members of cooperatives are other categories assimilated with employees. Under the WW (other than under the ZW and the WIA apprentices are not insured.

102. Article 5 of the employee insurance Acts empowers the Minister of Social Affairs and Employment to assimilate certain work relationships with employed persons by way of a decree. The following work relationships are mentioned: homeworkers and their assistants, musicians, artists, professional sportsmen and – as a residual category – the person who carries out work personally for a remuneration and whose work relationship is not considered as employment on the basis of the above-mentioned definitions but may be put on a par with it from a social point of view.

103. Articles 1 and 2 of this Decree provide that the work relationship of a homeworker and his assistant is considered as that of an employed person if the work relationship was entered into for at least thirty days and the gross income, as a rule, amounts to at least 40% of the statutory minimum wage. Article 4 of the measure includes musicians and other performing artists in the concept of employed person, without requirements on income or amount of work. Article 4(a) does the same for top sportsmen if they receive an allowance from the Ministry of Health and Sports for their living. Article 5(a) includes persons working as sex workers (prostitutes, etc.).

104. Article 5 of the Decree defines when a person belonging to the residual category is deemed to have a work relationship equivalent to that of an employed person. The first requirement is that the person in question carries out activities during, as a rule, at least two days a week. The third paragraph of Article 5 adds that the requirements that the work relationship should be entered into for at least thirty days and that the gross income should, generally, amount to at least 40% of the statutory minimum wage, must be met.

105. Article 4 mentions the assimilation of a person performing a job on the basis of a contract of assignment with an employed person provided he is not self-employed. *Supra*, in paragraph 116, we discussed that by means of the VAR-declaration it was made clear who was considered self-employed or not. However, now this declaration has been repealed and the succeeding act, DBA, is suspended this criterion remains a source for uncertainty. The policy seems to be to continue as in the old way – so generously assuming that a person is self-employed – unless it is clear that abuse is made of the situation.

106. Up to now we have discussed sections of the law in which the concept of employed person was decisive for who is covered by compulsory insurance and who is not. By defining which work relationships are considered as employed persons' relationships, the group of insured persons, i.e., employees, is determined. A different method is adopted in Articles 7, 8 and 8(a) and 8(b) of the ZW, Articles 8 and 9 WIA and Article 8 of the WW. These Articles define directly – and not on the basis of the concept of employed person – who is (also) considered to be an employee or, where appropriate, an insured person. These rules are relevant to persons who do not work and who (might) receive benefits on account of unemployment, sickness or disability.

C. Limitation of the Concept of Employed Person

107. The employee insurance Acts provide that certain work relationships are not considered as employed persons' relationships. These include the work relationships of:

- persons who perform particular offices as defined in the Acts (e.g., Minister, Ombudsman);
- persons who carry out activities with or without pay for a municipal fire brigade or as a police officer;

- persons who carry out exclusively (or almost exclusively) household or personal duties in the household, usually during less than four days a week, for a natural person by whom he is employed.

§2. Calculation of Contributions

I. Calculation Base

108. The contribution due by the person who is liable under the employee insurance Acts amounts to a percentage of the wages paid by the employer to the employee on account of the contract (of employment) made by them. The next paragraph will explain what is understood by wages. The Wet FSV is the main source for answering that question. This Act fits in closely with the description of the wage concept in the Tax on Wages Act in order to facilitate as much as possible the administration of employers who have to deduct both contributions and tax on wages and pay this to the Tax Office.

109. Article 16 Wet FSV refers to the definition of wage in the Act on Wage Tax for the purpose of application of the Wet FSV. Some forms of income are excluded from the wage concept for the Wet FSV, such as income from a previous job, unless provided otherwise in the Act.

110. Article 17 of the Wet FSV defines the upper limit of the wage upon which contributions can be levied. In 2016 the amount was EUR 203.85 per working day (EUR 52,766 a year).

II. Contribution Rates

A. Wet Werk en Inkomen Naar Arbeidsvermogen

111. Since 1998 a distinction has to be made under the WIA between differentiated and basic contributions. Both contributions have to be paid by the employer and they are both levied over wages received by the employee.

112. The differentiated contribution is paid to the Disability Differentiated Fund that is controlled and administered by the Uwv. Disability benefits are paid from this fund during a period of five years as of the day entitlement to the benefit arises. Since the differentiated contribution was not introduced until 1 January 1998, only the benefits effective as of that date are paid from differentiated contributions. The basic contribution is paid to the Disability Basic Fund that is also controlled and administered by the National Social Insurance Institution. All other payments and benefits within the framework of the Disability Insurance Act are paid from this fund.

1. The Differentiated Contribution Rate

113. The percentage of the differentiated contribution rate differs from one employer to another and depends on the costs of the employees of an employer who claimed disability benefits in the past five years.

114. The percentage is fixed by the Uwv for each individual employer.

115. The average contribution is 0.47%. For large employers (paying more than 3,140,000 a year on wages, the minimum rate is 0.12% and the maximum is 1.92% (2016).

2. The Rate of the Basic Contribution

116. The contribution percentage is determined by the Uwv subject to approval by the Minister of Social Affairs and Employment.

117. The basic contribution amounts to an equal percentage of wages for all sections of business and profession. The basic contribution for 2016 has been fixed at 5.88% of the employee's wages (subject to the ceiling discussed *supra*).

B. Werkloosheidswet

118. The contribution due for the WW is divided into a part that is paid to the unemployment benefit fund of the section of the economy to which the employer belongs and a part which is paid to the General Unemployment Fund. For each section of the economy, there is one unemployment fund, and the sections are defined by the Minister of Social Affairs and Employment.

119. The unemployment benefit funds and the General Unemployment Fund are controlled and administered by the Uwv. The employer, not the employee, has to pay the contributions to the unemployment benefit fund. The contribution that is paid to the General Unemployment Fund is to be paid by both the employer and the employee. Both types of contributions are collected by the Tax Office.

120. Benefits paid in the case of unemployment due to bad weather and the unemployment benefits over the first six months of unemployment to employees who have been working in a particular sector during the last six months before they became unemployed are paid from the unemployment fund of that same sector. In addition, the sick pay of the categories of persons mentioned in paragraph 269 under items (a) through (c) is paid out of the unemployment funds. Also some other specified expenses are paid from these funds, such as the administration costs for the payment of the benefits meant in this paragraph. All other benefits in connection with the Unemployment Benefits Act and the ZW are paid out of the General Unemployment Fund.

121. The Uwv determines the level of the contributions to be paid to the unemployment funds. Since the unemployment and bad weather risks vary according to the sectors of business and profession, the contribution percentages vary from one fund to another. The actual rates can be found on www.uwv.nl.

122. The percentage of the contribution payable to the General Unemployment Fund is also determined by the Uwv. This percentage is the same for all sectors of business and profession. For 2016 the rate is 2.07%, to be paid by employers only.

§3. Reductions and Exemptions

123. As mentioned in paragraph 134, Article 17 of the Wet FSV sets a limit to the amount of wages subject to contribution. If the wages per day are more than at least EUR 203.85 a day (2016), the surplus amount is disregarded for the calculation of the contributions for the WIA and the WW.

124. As mentioned in paragraph 113, the differentiated contribution rate for the WIA depends on recent disability benefits claims of the employees working for a particular employer. This risk is calculated by taking the amount paid in disability benefits for employees who were working for the employer in question when the disability started. The benefits of those who were disabled at the time that they entered employment (*see* paragraph 271) are not included at any rate if the person involved has remained disabled and if, as from the starting date of his employment, a period of six years has not elapsed. In other words, the employer does not have to pay an increase in the differentiated contribution. Essentially, this is a reduction of the differentiated contribution.

125. A further deviation from the contribution rules applies for so-called marginal work taken up by a beneficiary. The rules on contribution exemptions for marginal work are found in Article 50 Wet FSV. This Article provides that at his request, an employer may be exempted by the Uwv from payment of contribution due from both employer and employee for the employee insurance schemes of a person in receipt of benefit who is employed for not more than six consecutive weeks (during this period his benefit is reduced or terminated according to the applicable benefit rules, *see* subsequent chapters). Exemption is granted on condition that the employer did not previously employ the person in question during that calendar year and, moreover, that no exemption was granted for employing that particular person in that calendar year. By beneficiary is meant a person who, before the start of this employment of six weeks, received exclusively a Wwb, IOAW, or IOAZ benefit (public assistance), WW benefit (unemployment benefit), or WIA, WAO or Wajong benefit, and he must be registered at the Uwv WERKbedrijf.

126. Article 52 of Wet FSV provides that this exemption applies also for employers in the tobacco processing and agricultural sectors. They can be exempted, upon their request, from contributions for categories of persons, as defined in a decree, who do not receive benefits and who are not dependent on income from employment and who are not a beneficiary. Examples are school pupils, students and housewives.

127. There is also a reduction for contributions in case an employer recruits an employee of 56 years and over; in that case, he has a reduction EUR 7,000 for a full-time worker.

128. If an employer recruits a person in receipt of a specified disability benefit (and assimilated categories), as defined in Article 49 Wet FSV, his contribution are reduced contributions for the first three years of employment of this person.

The same rule applies in case a disabled person resumes work (his own work or different work) with his own employer, partially or completely, but this time the maximum duration is one year. The reduction also applies for persons who are disabled for less than 35% at the end of the waiting period of two years for disability benefit, who did not have an employment relationship with an employer other than his own during the last thirteen weeks of this waiting period and who is not able to do his own or suitable work for his own employer. A last condition is that the employee resumes work within five years after the end of the said waiting period for disability benefit.

The reduction on contributions is EUR 7,000 a year. Lower reductions apply for persons who do not have a full-time job (Article 50 Wet FSV).

129. As is the case for national insurance schemes, special rules apply for persons who have conscientious objections to insurance; the rules are found in Article 64 Wet FSV and were already discussed above.

§4. Opting Out

130. The WIA (Articles 82 et seq.) offers employers the opportunity to bear the risk of paying disability benefits themselves for employees who were employed by them on the first day of the waiting period for disability benefits.

131. This so-called own-risk rule involves the benefit administration (Uwv) deciding on the claim for disability benefit according to the applicable statutory rules, so the employer cannot reduce his risk by applying his own criteria for benefits. If benefits are awarded, the employer can, however, dispute a decision in a procedure before Uwv and also before court. However, the main way in which he should reduce the risk is by offering suitable work and measures that keep the person who becomes ill from becoming disabled.

132. The employer has to pay the costs of the disability benefit for a period of ten years for each of his employees who claim disability benefits.

Special rules apply in case an employee has more than one employer, in case an employer refuses to pay disability benefit and in case of transfer of enterprise; the rules can be found in the Wet FSV (Articles 82 et seq.).

The advantage of becoming an own-risk bearer is that the employer concerned does not have to pay the differentiated contribution of the WIA for his employees.

§5. Contributions on Benefit Payments

133. Employees insurance and national insurance schemes contributions have also to be paid on employee insurance benefits (i.e., unemployment, illness or disability benefits), as provided by Article 16 Wet FSV. The Uwv has to deduct these contributions from the benefit and pay the employers' contributions to the Tax Office.

§6. Contributions for the Voluntary Insurance

134. Under certain conditions it is possible to take out voluntary insurance. These conditions are listed in Article 64 of the ZW, in Articles 18 through 21(a) of the WIA and in Articles 53 through 60 of the WW.

135. These provisions give the right to persons belonging to specified categories to enter voluntary insurances. For example, the WIA includes persons whose compulsory insurance ended and for whom it can reasonably be assumed that the interruption of compulsory insurance will be for a short period only or if they are available for the labour market in the sense of Article 16 of the WW. Also, people who become self-employed and who have had compulsory insurance for one year can apply for admission to the voluntary insurance. The same applies for development-aid workers in specified projects in developing countries.

136. The group of persons eligible for voluntary insurance under the WW is smaller than that for the WIA, which is understandable given the nature of the WW. Voluntary insurance is possible for the WW only if the person concerned does not live in the Netherlands and adopts a job abroad for a maximum period of five years, or if a person works abroad and lives in the Netherlands, or for development-aid workers and persons working for international organizations.

137. The applicant for voluntary insurance determines the level of the daily wage he wishes to have insured at the start of the insurance. In other words, the claimant can determine the income he wishes to have insured. The contribution depends on the level of the thus insured income. The law mentions some upper limits to the part of the wage that can be insured: it must not be higher than the maximum daily wage relevant to compulsory insurance mentioned in the Wet FSV, and it cannot be more than the person, according to the assessment of the Uwv, will lose in case the risk materializes. The voluntary insurance contribution is fixed at a percentage of the daily wage. The benefit by virtue of the voluntary insurance is also calculated on the basis of the daily wage.

Chapter 3. National Insurance Schemes

§1. Who Is Liable to Pay Contributions?

138. The *Wet Financiering Sociale Verzekeringen* (Wet FSV [Social Insurance Schemes Financing Act]) provides, in Article 6, that the 'insured' person is liable to pay contributions for the national insurance schemes. In the specific laws that regulate each of the national insurance schemes, there is a definition of who are considered insured persons.

Insured persons are, according to these rules the following: (a) residents and (b) persons who are not residents, but who are subject to the Dutch Tax Law on Wages on the ground that they are employed in the Netherlands. The law limits the insurance to persons between specified age limits.

139. The laws give the Government the power to deviate by general Decree from the provisions mentioned under (a) and (b); it can extend or restrict the group of insured persons. On the basis of these powers, the Government has adopted a general legislative measure outlining such extensions and restrictions.

140. In making such extensions and restrictions, the Government is not entirely free, since it has to take into consideration the obligations resulting from international treaties and EU regulations (such as Regulation 883/2004).

141. Persons who are compulsorily insured for the Wlz are also compulsorily insured for the Zvw. In other words, the definitions of residents for the national insurance schemes are also relevant to this law. Residents are, however, not *ex lege* covered by insurance under the Zvw, but they have to choose a particular insurance of an insurance company, and they have to pay contributions for this insurance to this company. Fines apply, as determined by the Zvw, if people do not insure themselves. Since the matter is, therefore, mainly a private matter, the following rules do not apply for Zvw contributions.

142. In 1998 an Act came into force, the *Koppelingswet* (Benefit Entitlement (Residence Status) Act), which inserted a provision into the national insurance schemes which reads that a foreigner is not insured under these schemes if he has not been admitted unconditionally (in the sense of Article 8(a–e) and (l) of the *Vreemdelingenwet* (Aliens Act) to the Netherlands. Exceptions to this principle can be made by a general legislative measure.

143. Residents are those who live in the Netherlands. From the case law it follows that the question of where a person lives has to be determined on the basis of the circumstances of the case. As a general requirement, there have to be ties of a social and economic nature between the person concerned and the Netherlands. This requirement means that the person concerned has to both contribute to this community and be dependent upon it. Whether this is the case has to be determined on the basis of the facts. Few statutory provisions can be found on this issue; most of the criteria were developed in the case law.

144. Special rules concern persons working on ships and aircrafts for whom the Netherlands is their home port. The ships and aircrafts are considered to be part of the Netherlands as far as their crews are concerned. In addition, someone who has left and later returned to the Netherlands within one year, and who meanwhile has not lived in the Dutch Antilles, Aruba or the territory of another State, is considered to have lived in the Netherlands for the duration of his absence. The assessment of who is a resident in addition to having a tie with the Netherlands becomes more complicated when a person also has a tie with another country. In that case, it has to be determined whether the bond with the Netherlands is so strong that this particular person has to be considered a resident here. It is possible that there are such strong ties with both the Netherlands and another country that a particular person can be considered to have more than one place of residence. This may be the case if a foreigner starts working in the Netherlands and leaves his family in the country of origin, or if a Dutch person goes to work abroad while his family stays in the Netherlands. Circumstances in which it may be determined whether someone is living in the Netherlands include the following: having a residence permit, the duration of the stay, the place of work, being registered in the civil registries, having a place to live, maintaining contacts with (Dutch) people and institutions, and having a bank account in the Netherlands. All these social and economic circumstances have to be taken into account.

145. Non-residents can be insured in the Netherlands if they are subject to the Dutch Law on Tax on Wages on the grounds that they are employed in the Netherlands. This stipulation reflects the 'country of employment principle', a principle that is consistent with Article 11(2) of Regulation 883/2004. This provision is based on the economic ties of the person concerned to the Netherlands. Examples of persons satisfying this condition are those who work in the Netherlands and live in Belgium or Germany. Under Article 1 of the Tax on Wages Act, a person is liable to tax on wages and therefore insured under the national insurance schemes if he is employed by an employer who is liable to withhold tax from his income. This means that the employer has to reside or be established in the Netherlands, with a fixed place of business or a permanent representative here. It can also be the case that the employer concerned is appointed by the minister as the person who is liable to withhold tax.

146. Extension and limitation of the group of insured persons under the national insurance scheme are regulated in a general decree.[11] The main purpose of this decree is to extend or restrict the compulsory insurance for certain categories. The coverage is extended to categories of residents on the grounds that they only temporarily live abroad or that they still receive their wages from the Netherlands. Excluded from coverage may be, among other categories, foreign diplomats.

When interpreting the Decree which defines the extension or restriction of the personal scope of the national insurance schemes, international regulations and treaties have to be taken into account, in particular EU Regulation 883/2004.

147. Article 22 of the Decree empowers the SVB to grant exemption from insurance for the national insurance schemes to a person at this person's request, subject to certain conditions (in particular, that he is already covered by a foreign scheme). Furthermore, Article 24 authorizes the bank to deviate from the rules of the decree in

11. *Besluit uitbreiding en beperking kring verzekerden volksverzekering 1999*, as amended.

case of hardship exclusively resulting from compulsory insurance or exclusion from insurance on the basis of the decree.

§2. Calculation of the Contributions

148. The calculation of contributions has to take place according to the rules of the Wet FSV. For insured persons who are self-employed, the income which is subject to contributions is the same income that is subject to tax or is the income subject to tax as defined in the Income Tax Act. The insured person has to submit a tax form of his income to the Tax Office and subsequently receives an assessment, i.e., a statement of the amount he has to pay.

149. For insured persons who are employed persons, the income which is subject to contributions is the same as the wage defined in the Tax on Wages Act. The employer withholds the national insurance contributions from the wages and transfers them to the Tax Office. This Office collects the amount of contributions to be paid and, upon receipt of this sum, pays it to the relevant funds for financing the various social security benefits.

150. The contribution rate is a percentage that is applied on the income as defined in the previous paragraph, currently (2016) the maximum income liable for these contributions is EUR 33,715.

151. Also social security benefits are treated as income from which contributions are to be deducted.

152. The contribution percentage is determined by a decree of the Minister of Social Affairs and Employment for the old-age pensions (AOW) and survivors pensions (Anw); the maximum contribution for old-age pensions is 18.25% on the applicable income (if there is a deficit, this has to be paid from taxes). In 2016 the actual rate was 17.90 (maximum EUR 5,972 per year). For the Anw there is no maximum on contributable income laid down in the Law. In 2016 the rate was 0.6% (max EUR 200 per year).

153. The contribution rate for the Wlz is determined by two ministers, *viz.*, the Minister of Welfare, Health and Sports and the Minister of Social Affairs and Employment. In 2016 the rate was 9.65% (max EUR 4,220 per year).

154. The boards of the Funds responsible for the benefits concerned have to estimate how much money they will need to cover the costs in the next year. Together with an estimate of the income that is expected in the same year in connection with work, this will constitute the data necessary to determine the contribution percentage. Obviously, it is not possible to achieve an accurate balance between annual income and expenditure in this way. Moreover, there are several reasons why it would be wise to build up a reserve for the funds. In the first place, such a reserve could be used to prevent too big an increase in the contribution percentage in a subsequent year when expenditure suddenly rises faster. Second, the reserve can provide the necessary liquid assets. It should be invested in such a way that money can be withdrawn at short notice. The funds may borrow money from each other or on the money market.

§3. Contribution Reductions and Exemptions

155. Not the entire wage or income from work is subject to contributions. The law defines which deductions apply; there are general deductions and also deductions for particular categories. In addition there is a limit, as already mentioned, to the amount of income to be taken into account.

In principle each resident over the age of 15 has to pay contributions. Nearly all social security benefits are considered as income under this legislation. The Wet FSV allows for a few exceptions only. People who are over pension age no longer have to pay contributions for the AOW. The pension age is gradually decreasing.

156. Some persons belonging to particular groups in the Dutch society (mainly radically Christian religious communities) have conscientious objections to be covered by social security, since these are seen as interfering with the effects of fate that was determined by God. If one has such conscientious objections to one or more national insurance schemes or employees insurance schemes, Article 64 of the Wet FSV offers the possibility to request exemption from obligations imposed on those who are liable to pay contribution in accordance with this Act. This concerns persons who object to taking out insurances, both private and imposed ones, for reasons of principle in connection with their religious beliefs. At their request, these persons may be exempted from paying contribution. Instead of contributions they have to pay extra income tax or tax on wages for the same amount as the applicable contributions, but they are not covered by the insurance schemes. So it is entirely a matter of conscience.

§4. Voluntary Insurance Contributions

157. In a number of cases, (formerly) insured persons can take out voluntary insurance on the basis of the national insurance schemes for the periods between the ages of 15 and pension age if they were not compulsorily insured during that time. This is especially important for people who temporarily live or lived outside the Netherlands and who can or could not be insured sufficiently abroad. The AOW and the Anw (General Survivors Pension Act) have this possibility. The rules can be found in the AOW, Anw and Wet FSV.

158. Voluntary insurance is possible for a person who has been compulsorily insured for at least one year for a maximum period of ten years, starting immediately after the last day of compulsory insurance. The AOW (Article 35) allows for some exceptions to the maximum period of ten years (e.g., for persons doing development aid). Voluntary insurance can be requested only by persons under the age of 65. Voluntary insurance is possible if the person concerned notifies the SVB within one year of the ending of the compulsory insurance that he wants to participate in the voluntary insurance.

§5. Administration

159. The national insurance contributions are levied by the Tax Office. This Office forwards an assessment to the person liable to pay contribution. If the person liable to pay contributions is subject to tax on wages, the national insurance contributions are levied in accordance with the regulations that apply to the collection of tax on wages. If the person liable to pay contributions receives an assessment, the contributions that have been withheld will be deducted in the final assessment.

160. The Tax Office collects the contributions in the same way as the collection of income tax and tax on wages. This means that, in case the person liable to pay fails to do so, the Office can take measures. The Tax Office transfers the contribution revenues collected to the Old Age Pension Fund and the Survivors' Pension Fund, which are administered by the SVB and to the Wlz Fund, which is administered by the CVZ.

Chapter 4. State Funding

161. In principle, the benefits payable by insurance schemes are paid from contributions only.

162. An exception is that the State contributes to the financing of the AOW (General Old-Age Pension Law) in case the present contribution of 17.90% is insufficient to cover the cost charged to the old-age pension fund.

163. In order to be able to finance the expenses of the AOW benefits in the future, a fund was created. Every year sums from the national budget are paid to this fund, which is controlled by the Minister of Social Affairs and Employment. The sum is determined by this Minister and the Minister of Finance. It is not be possible to charge expenditures on behalf of the general old-age pension insurance to the savings fund before 2020; this protects the fund against early claims.

164. The costs of the child benefits are paid from the State budget. Also public assistance benefits are – sometimes indirectly – paid by the State, although local communities sometimes have their own responsibilities.

Part III. Health Care

Chapter 1. Introduction

165. Medical expenses constitute a risk which practically nobody can bear without insurance. For a long time, the Government kept its distance with regard to laying down regulations covering medical expenses. Up until the Second World War, medical insurance was almost exclusively in the hands of private companies. Government involvement in this field was confined to the medical and surgical treatment provided under the *Ongevallenwet* (Industrial Accident Act) to those who had suffered an industrial accident. Medical care to the poor could be provided under the Poor Law.

166. In 1941 the *Ziekenfondsbesluit* (Health Insurance Decree) was adopted, the first compulsory insurance scheme for medical expenses. This Decree provided for benefits in kind and prevented the insured person from incurring the cost of medical care. Initially, the scope of the regulation was restricted to low-wage employees and their families. After the Second World War, more and more categories of persons with low income were included in the scheme. At the same time, the list of provisions payable on the basis of this Act increased. In 1966 the ZFB was replaced with the Zfw which was basically not very different from its predecessor: it insured employed persons with an income below a specified ceiling.

167. Two years later, in 1968, the AWBZ Act was introduced. Where the Zfw aimed at covering the more 'ordinary' medical expenses, the AWBZ covers those risks which, generally speaking, cannot or can hardly be covered by private insurance. The AWBZ is a national insurance scheme which, in principle, is applicable to all residents of the Netherlands.

168. A typical characteristic of the Zfw was that a great many persons were not covered by this Act, in particular employees earning an income above the threshold, self-employed persons and civil servants. These persons had to buy private medical insurance for those medical expenses that are not covered by the AWBZ. More than 30% of the Dutch population had to resort to private insurance companies to cover the risk of ordinary medical expenses.

169. In 2006 a new Law came into force, the Zvw. This Act covers all residents and as a result the 'gap' of coverage by the predecessor, the Zfw, does not exist anymore.

Chapter 2. The Zorgverzekeringswet

§1. Field of Application

I. Territorial Field of Application

170. The Zvw is a national insurance scheme that covers all residents. This Act was deemed necessary, since the increase of technology and the greying of the population meant that costs of medical care are expected to grow continuously. The Zvw is supposed to have some built-in elements which can control the costs easier: the Act is to be administered by private insurance companies, and the role of the State is more limited. The Act itself defines the contents of the basis insurance and thus ensures basic protection of the insured. Sections I and II below deal with the group of insured persons and the way they are covered.

II. Personal Field of Application

171. The Zvw provides that persons who are insured under the Wlz and the regulations based on this Act are obliged to buy a health insurance. In other words, persons covered by the Act are not insured *ex lege* but have the obligation to insure themselves.

172. By referring to the personal scope of the Wlz, the Zvw covers all residents and persons subject to wage tax in the Netherlands. We discussed the concept of resident in paragraph 85.

173. The term 'regulations based on the Wlz' in paragraph 169 refers to the *Besluit uitbreiding en beperking kring verzekerden volksverzekeringen* (Decree extension and restriction of insured persons for national insurances), which Decree extends and restricts the personal scope, e.g., by covering students temporarily studying abroad and excluding students temporarily studying in the Netherlands.

174. Under the Zfw, family members of insured persons who were not insured on basis of an employment relationship were still covered by this Act; they were called co-insured persons. Under the Zvw all residents are covered, so co-insurance does not exist anymore.

175. A special position still exists for family members of persons who work but do not reside in the Netherlands. They are covered by the Zvw on the basis of international regulations, including Regulation 883/2004.

Family members who are covered as a result of the application of Regulation 883/2004 have to register with Zorginstituut Nederland and have to pay a contribution to this organization.

176. The Zvw covers a much larger group than the Zvw, as the Zvw includes also self-employed persons and others who are not employed persons and it covers persons regardless of their income.

177. Also pensioners who receive a Dutch pension and reside in another country feel the results of the new Act. If they receive a pension from the Netherlands only, they are covered by the Zvw and they have to pay contributions in the Netherlands.

In the past, this was true only if they were covered by the Zfw, i.e., if they were low-wage earners before they became pensioners. Many pensioners contested this change, but it follows from the application of Articles 28 et seq. of Regulation 1408/71, the predecessor of Regulation 883/2004, which defines by which health insurance scheme pensioners are covered, that their coverage (and therefore the obligation to pay contributions) is inescapable.[12]

178. A person who is within the personal scope of the Zvw is obliged to buy an insurance from a private insurance company. Health insurance is on offer from a large number of companies. They (have to) offer basically the same basic insurance, i.e., the basic contents is specified by law (although there may be differences in the extent of the choice insured persons have in care provider) and policies may offer more than the basic contents.

179. The companies have to determine the contribution rates for their insurance and that is their major instrument of competition. Another element in the competition is the additional, voluntary insurance they offer in addition to the basic insurance. The additional insurance may be so attractive that persons chose the insurance company's basic insurance.

180. Insurance companies can offer deductions for participants of a collective contract for a basic insurance to a maximum of 10%. There are no limitations on which institutions or organizations can make a collective contract with an insurance company. Employers are often in a position to make a collective contract, but also organizations of patients and even sport clubs can do so. The reductions in contributions that are realized in this way are, in practice, a very important factor in choosing insurance. This means that employees often choose the company with which their employer has made a collective contract.

181. Health insurance companies may not refuse anyone for the basic insurance (in other words, they are obligated to accept all applicants). Contributions for the basic insurance must be the same for all buyers of a particular policy, thus they must not be linked to the state of health of individual clients. Contribution differentiation is thus banned.

§2. Benefits

I. General

182. Articles 10 and 11 of the Zvw define the provisions to which insured persons are entitled according to the law, i.e., the basic insurance. As discussed

12. Court of Justice 14 Oct. 2010, Case C-345/09, *Van Delft.*

previously, the insurance company can add provisions to the basic insurance. It can also offer a supplementary insurance. The company itself fixes the contribution rate and must, therefore, calculate which combination of price and provision is competitive enough.

183. Article 10 of the Zvw defines the insured risk as follows: medical care; dental care; pharmaceutical care; aids and instruments; nursing; stay in a hospital; and transport for medical treatment.

184. Article 11 mentions the duty to give care, which is elaborated in the *Besluit zorgverzekering* (Decision on the care insurance), based on the Zvw, in large detail. In essence, it means that the basic insurance includes the following:

- medical care, as provided by General Practitioners (GP), obstetricians, medical specialists and clinical psychologists;
- admission to and treatment/nursing in hospitals;
- ambulance, transport by taxi or public transport;
- drugs;
- medical aids, e.g., hearing aids, elastic stockings and incontinence-related products;
- maternity care;
- dental care (only up to the age of 22); and
- paramedical care, e.g., physiotherapy, logopaedics and dietary advice.

II. Conditions

185. In order to be entitled to benefits under the Zvw, a person must have bought insurance and satisfied the conditions of the insurance.

186. A condition for entitlement to a particular provision is often that the health insurance has given a prior permission. This is the case, for example, for most additional aids and often also for paramedical care.

187. Entitlement to a provision often only exists after prescription by a doctor. For instance, non-clinical specialist care can only be received upon referral by a GP. Paramedical care is only given after referral by a GP or a specialist. Entitlement to ambulance service only exists on the orders of the physician in attendance. Many drugs (pharmaceutical care) are only supplied on the basis of a prescription by the physician who treats the person concerned.

188. For some types of provisions, cost sharing by the patient is required. The situations in which cost sharing applies are mentioned in a Decree.

III. Benefits in Cash or in Kind

189. The health insurance conditions can have two main approaches: (a) they can define that the provisions are in kind and the care providers to which a patient can go; or (b) they can provide that the costs of treatment are reimbursed and that the patient thus has maximum freedom. The latter system is more attractive but will also mean a higher contribution for the insurance.

Chapter 3. Wet Langdurige zorg ('Longterm Care Act')

§1. Field of Application

I. Territorial Field of Application

190. The Wlz, which dates from 2015, is the successor of the AWBZ. The change was deemed necessary since the scope of the AWBZ had been extended through time and was no longer limited to exceptional expenses (i.e., expenses that cannot be borne by an individual, that are not insurable). The Wlz now focuses on a care again, and `more precisely on persons who need, in a care institution, care and supervision during day and night. In order to be eligible a so-called indication of the Centrale Indicatiestelling Zorg is required. The provisions of the AWBZ that are not transferred to the Wlz, may be covered by the Zvw or the *Wet maatschappelijke zorg* (WMO [Act on social care]), although strict conditions apply, which may mean that for particular care one has to rely on relatives first.

II. Personal Field of Application

191. The Wlz is a national insurance scheme. The group of insured persons is formed by residents of the Netherlands. Also insured are those persons who do not reside in the Netherlands but who are subject to tax on wages because they are employed in the Netherlands. The group of persons covered was discussed in paragraphs 83 et seq.

§2. Benefits

I. General

192. On the basis of the Wlz, insured persons are entitled to care that is defined in Article 3.1.1 of the Act. This includes staying in an institution providing medical care, personal treatment, pharmaceutical care, dental care, transport, but only if the conditions are satisfied mentioned in the Act and the Scheme long-term care. The condition is that the insured person reasonably needs the care, but he also has to rely on this since, because of a somatic or psychogeriatric disability, or restriction or mental or physical handicap needs permanent supervision or needs twenty-four hours a day care. The various types of care under the law will be discussed in paragraph 194.

193. Insurance companies are obliged to see to it that persons with a policy of their company can assert their rights to care. In order to meet this obligation, they enter into contracts with persons and institutions which are able to provide one or more types of care included in the care package (care providers).

An insured person who wishes to assert his rights to care must apply to one of the care providers contracted by his insurer, which will then provide the appropriate care. If this concerns care in the form of benefits in kind, the insured person receives the care in kind as defined in the contract the insurance company made with the care provider. The contracted provider is paid directly by the insurer.

194. The following types of care are included in the Wlz (Article 3.3.1):

- staying in an institution providing medical care;
- personal treatment and nursing;
- pharmaceutical care;
- dental care;
- clothing related to the character and aim of the institution;
- transport to the place where the person is treated.

A. Conditions

195. The care provided by the Wlz is subject to certain conditions. An important condition is that there are medical grounds for giving the care as defined by the Centraal Indicatieorgaan Zorg (CIZ, Central Indication body for care). This is a foundation that decides what type of a care a person needs, given his physical or physical situation (paragraph 199). The indication decision provides whether a person needs care, and if so, in which form and extent. Without this decision he cannot get care on the basis of the Wlz.

196. The CIZ has to investigate which care a person needs, i.e., the care that fits best with his situation. This may mean that the CIZ has to investigate whether the person needs care in addition to that which is requested. The investigation by the CIZ does not only involve that of the personal situation of the claimant, but also the circumstances in which he lives and the social circumstances. This may also mean that if a person can get help from, for instances, his family, then he may need less care on the basis of the Wlz.

197. The indication decision is subject to review and appeal procedures.

B. Forms of Care

198. Under the Wlz insured persons can choose between care in kind and a so-called individual personal budget. In case an insured person desires to receive care in kind he has to contact a care provider contracted by his insurance company and in case of a non-contracted one he has to ask permission. In case the patient contacts a foreign care provider, the rules apply as following from the Cross border patient direct (2011/24). The personal budget allows the patient to organize the care he needs on his own terms. The budgets give much more freedom to patients than possible in case of care in kind, since the individual can make an agreement with a care provider on the desired care. In this way the care can be adjusted to the wishes of the individual.

199. The decisions on the budgets are taken by the CIZ. The CIZ assesses which treatment a person needs and the level of the budget depends on this.

200. The CIZ sends the decision to the benefit administration of the Wlz, which decides on the budget available for the treatment.

201. As already stated, the budgets are beneficial for the freedom of choice of the claimants. If a person needs help, he can choose his own care provider with whom he can make an agreement. Such an agreement can also be made with family members or friends and they can be paid from the budget. Such relationship allows the patient to make professional arrangements with the care provider, which may make him less dependent and will give him more room to decide on his own affairs. The patient can also agree with the care provider on the wage to be paid, taking account, of course, statutory rules, e.g., on minimum wages. Such contracts have to be in writing; examples of such contracts are provided by supporting organizations.[13]

C. Own Contributions

202. In many cases, cost sharing by the patient is a condition for obtaining care. This is laid down in the Besluit langdurige zorg (Decision on long-term care).

203. The level of the contribution depends on the level of the income and capital of the patient and, if he is married, on the income of his partner.

13. Per saldo, www.pgb.nl (accessed on 11 Dec. 2012).

Part IV. Family Allowances

Chapter 1. Introduction

204. Family benefits are payable on the basis of the AKW. Since 1980 this has been the only Act on child benefits. Before this year there were various regulations for various population groups.

205. The AKW covers all residents of the Netherlands and is administered by one organization, the SVB. In 1986, a major change took place when students ages 18 and older were excluded as persons for whom child benefits are payable; they receive study grants instead. If students are parents, they can receive child benefits for their own children.

Chapter 2. Child Benefits

§1. Field of Application

206. The AKW provides that only insured persons are entitled to child benefit. The Act still uses the term 'insured persons', even though the AKW is not a real insurance scheme anymore, as no contribution is levied for benefits payable on the basis of this Act. Since 1989, child benefit has been financed entirely from taxes.

207. The group of insured persons is determined in the same way as for national insurance schemes. The first category of compulsorily insured persons is formed by residents. The second category is made up of those who are not residents, but who are subject to tax on wage as a result of the fact that they are employed in the Netherlands (Article 6 AKW). The group of persons covered by national insurance schemes (and the AKW) has been dealt with before (paragraphs 83 et seq.).

§2. Conditions for Child Benefits

I. General

208. The main conditions for entitlement to child benefit are listed in Article 7(1) and (2), of the AKW, which read as follows:

(1) In accordance with the provisions of this Act, the insured person is entitled to child benefits for his own children, stepchildren and foster children who:

(a) are under the age of 16 and belong to his household;
(b) are under the age of 18 and are supported by him to a considerable extent.

(2) The insured person is entitled to child benefit for children of 16 or 17 years of age, provided those children:

(a) are fulfilling the obligations of the Act on compulsory education (i.e., there is no truancy, i.e., for more than sixteen hours in four successive weeks) or are exempted from these (e.g., in case of disability) in order to get a so-called start qualification (completing secondary school). This start qualification is a qualification level that is deemed necessary to enter the labour market in order to have better chances to get work; only when such a qualification is obtained one is no longer subject to compulsory education, and if the child cannot find work he is accepted as unemployed for this Act; or
(b) are attending school abroad comparable with that required by the Act on compulsory education; or

(c) are unemployed and registered with Uwv WERKbedrijf.

209. Article 11 of the AKW provides that these conditions have to be met on the first day of the calendar quarter (thus 1 January, 1 April, 1 July, 1 October). An insured person who meets the conditions on that day (the reference date) is entitled to child benefit for the whole calendar quarter of which this day is the first day.

210. There are, however, exceptions to the rule that the conditions have to be satisfied on the first day of the quarter only. The most important exception is that when answering the question whether an insured person sufficiently supports a child (paragraphs 210 et seq.), the support during the whole calendar quarter is taken into account and not only on the first day.

211. An insured person who lives outside the Netherlands on the reference date is, in principle, not entitled to family benefits – an exception is when he is subject to wage tax in the Netherlands or that under EU Regulation 883/2004 he is subject to Dutch law. An insured person cannot claim child benefits either for children who are living outside the Netherlands on the reference date unless the conditions mentioned below are met. In this respect, a stay of more than three months abroad is equated with living outside the Netherlands. These exclusions do not apply when a treaty is made between the Netherlands and the country in which the insured person or child resides. This includes the countries within the territorial scope of Regulation 883/2004.

212. The exclusion from benefit entitlement does not apply if the insured person or the child lives outside the Netherlands but stays in the Netherlands for a continuous period of more than three months (Article 7(b)).

II. The Definition of Child

213. An insured person can claim child benefit only for his own children, his stepchildren and his foster children.

214. By the term 'own children', the insured person's legitimate and natural children are meant.

III. Which Children Are Eligible?

215. An insured person cannot claim child benefit for children over 18. These children are supposed to be able to support themselves by income from employment, benefits or allowances such as study grants.

216. The largest category of children for whom child benefit may be claimed is formed by children under the age of 16 who belong to the insured person's household. In general, if there is a family (husband, wife, children) there is also a household. A household is a social and economic unit with a permanent residence. A temporary absence of the child because of a holiday or admission to a hospital will not sever the ties with the household.

217. The SVB has elaborated policy rules on many topics of the laws it administers, to be found on its website (in Dutch). In respect of the term 'household', it acknowledges that a person may have such ties with respect to the Netherlands and another country that it has to be concluded that he has two places of residence. This is relevant to determining whether a person who is a resident of the Netherlands also has a household with his children staying abroad. The policy rules for dealing with this issue are as follows. From the moment a person has become a resident of the Netherlands, he has such strong ties with this country that in principle it is accepted that these impede the assumption that he still has a place of residence in the country of origin. It can happen, however, that a resident of the Netherlands has such narrow ties to the country of origin that he can also be a resident of the country of origin. By the assessment of the question whether this is the case the criteria for residence, as discussed in previous sections, are relevant. This means that the legal, economic and social ties of the person concerned with the country of origin are assessed and that it is relevant that these ties are actually maintained by a long-term stay in the country of origin. This criterion of long-term stay is satisfied if the person concerned stays in the country of origin for more than three months yearly.

218. If the insured person does not have a household with his children, he has to satisfy support conditions in order to be entitled to child benefits for these children (*see* section IV below). Furthermore, there are special conditions for children ages 16 and 17. They have to go to secondary school or vocational training or have s start qualification in order to be eligible for child benefit.

219. The condition on education means that the child is following compulsory education (and there is no truancy) or when he is exempted from this, for instance because of disability. After he has obtained an initial qualification he may qualify if he is unemployed.

IV. The Support Requirement

220. If the insured person wishes to claim child benefits for children under the age of 16 who do not belong to his household, the person must satisfy the condition that he supports that child to a considerable degree. The support requirement also applies to persons who wish to claim child benefit for children ages 16 and 17. Regulations have been laid down in a decree on the basis of Article 7(4) of the AKW, in accordance with which it is assessed whether a child is supported to a considerable degree by the insured person.

221. Article 9 AKW provides that any income of the child is assumed to be used to support that child. What is to be understood by a child's income is stated in a ministerial regulation which was made on the basis of Article 9(2).

222. The main rule of the decree on the support requirements is that a child is assumed to be supported to a considerable degree by the insured person if the child's income does not exceed a certain amount. This is the case for a child of 16 and 17 age belonging to the household of the insured person if he earns less than EUR 1,266 net wage per calendar quarter (during the Summer quarter he can earn an additional EUR 1,300). If the child earns more than the mentioned amounts, there is no right to child benefit, even not if there are higher amounts needed for the household than normal. Sometimes it is not self-evident that the insured person supports the child. This is the case, for instance, if the child belongs to the household of the insured person's former spouse or if he stays in an institution. In order to answer the question whether the insured person supports the child to a considerable degree, it is not sufficient to set the requirement that the child's income not exceed a certain amount. If the insured person contributes at least EUR 416 per calendar quarter, he is assumed to maintain the child to 'an important extent'. The insured person has to prove these payments, for instance, by bank transfers to the person to which household the child belongs.

223. The insured person is also obliged to prove to the SVB that he makes this contribution towards supporting the child in each calendar quarter. As a cost of support is included the money paid in connection with the child's cost of living or its education. Cost of support also includes travelling expenses incurred by the insured person in order to visit the child who, due to illness or infirmity, does not belong to his household.

224. When investigating whether the insured person meets the support requirement contributions towards the child's support by others are also taken into account. Relevant are person(s) with whom the insured person forms a household and the person(s) who, by virtue of an agreement or a judicial decision, is obliged to contribute to the child's support.

§3. Amount of the Benefit

I. General

225. Before 1993, the level of the child benefit allowance was determined by the child's age and the size of the family to which it belonged. Between 1993 and 1995, the place of the child in the family (was he first, second, third, etc. child?) also formed a factor which determined the child benefit level. Since 1995, only the child's age is taken into account.

226. For a child under the age of 6, the amount is EUR 197 per calendar quarter; for children between the ages of 6 and 12 it is EUR 239 and it is EUR 282 for children over 12 but under 18. The child's age on the first day of the calendar quarter is decisive. As from July 2016 family benefit is 70% of the basic child benefit of EUR 273.89 per child younger than 6, 85% for a child younger than 12 and 100% for a child younger than 18. For children living outside the EU a correction related to the costs of living in the country where they live is replied.

II. Double Child Benefit

227. Under some conditions, children are counted twice for the purpose of determining the level of child benefit. This is the case with a child who does not belong to the insured person's household. For children under the age of 16, it is additionally required that the child concerned suffers from illness or infirmity or is engaged in an education or vocational training. Furthermore, the child must not belong to another person's household as his own child, stepchild or foster child. Finally, the child must be supported for a predominant part by the insured person (Article 7(5)).

III. Regulations Against Overlapping of Child Benefit

228. More than one person may be entitled to child benefits over the same period for the same children. Child benefits should be paid only once for each child, as is the legislator's understandable view, so it has to be determined to whom it is paid. If a woman and a man have a joint household, the choice is free. They may inform the SVB of their choice (Article 18(2)).

229. If they have not made a choice, the SVB decides to whom benefits are paid (Article 18(3)). If two or more persons, including the person to whose household the child belongs, are entitled to child benefits over the same period for the same child, child benefits are not paid to the person to whose household the child does not belong (Article 18(4)). In other cases of overlapping entitlements to child benefits, the benefits are paid to the person making the highest contribution towards the child's support. The others do not receive child benefit (Article 18(5)). In accordance with Article 18(6), a decree may set further rules for cases of overlapping, deviating from sections 4 and 5 of that Article. Parts of the benefits which have to be paid to an insured person can, on his request, be paid to other insured persons.

230. Article 20 deals with child benefits payable under the AKW overlapping with entitlement of child benefits on the basis of a regulation in another country. In order to prevent overlapping of child benefits, a ministerial regulation was laid down in 1985, stipulating that the Dutch child benefit will only be paid insofar as it exceeds the child benefit amount obtained by virtue of the regulation in the other country.

§4. Obligations

231. In accordance with the nature of the sanction, a distinction may be made between the general obligation of informing the benefit administration on relevant facts and the other obligations in the AKW. The sanction for violating the general obligation of informing the benefit administration is an administrative fine. The other obligations are not enforced by an administrative fine but by an administrative measure. This measure consists of the complete or partial, temporary or permanent refusal of child benefits.

I. The General Obligation to Provide Information

232. The insured person is obliged to inform the SVB at its request or immediately of his own accord of all facts and circumstances which he could reasonably assume might affect the entitlement to child benefits, the level of child benefits, the assertion of the right to child benefits or the child benefits amount which is paid (Article 15).

233. There is a fine for the violation of the general obligation of informing the SVB. Articles 17a and the following provide that the SVB is obliged to impose a fine if the relevant statutory obligations are not followed. Only in case of urgent reasons may the SVB decide not to impose a fine. The maximum fine is that of the amount by which the SVB was disadvantaged, but not lower than EUR 3,350. The SVB can refrain from imposing a fine, unless a previous warning has been given or a fine has been imposed within the last two years.

II. Obligations Enforced by Measures

234. Article 16 of the AKW stipulates that the SVB is authorized to lay down verification regulations and that the insured person is obliged to comply with these regulations. Among other things, these verification regulations provide that the person who wants to claim child benefits has to submit a written request to that extent and that he has to do this on a special form available from the SVB (Article 3 of the verification regulations). At the SVB's request, the person receiving or requesting child benefits will also use special forms to notify any changes (Article 5). The verification regulations further state, if required so by the SVB, that the child will undergo a medical examination at the request of the SVB to determine the child's incapacity to work (Article 6). In addition, the verification regulations contain rules on informing the SVB of changes in the social-fiscal number (now called *Burgerservicenummer*) of the insured person or a child (Article 4), on allowing access to inspect books, documents and other data carriers, on submitting valid proof of identity and a certificate of life if the person requesting child benefits or the child is living abroad (Article 7). The verification regulations also stipulate that the person receiving or requesting child benefits has to obey a summons to appear and to supply the necessary information (Article 8) and that he should enable verification (Article 9). Finally, the verification regulations state in detail what items of evidence (school certificates, medical certificates, pay slips pertaining to support contributions, proof of the child's income, etc.) have to be submitted (Articles 10 through 16).

235. The person who has violated the verification regulations is confronted with a measure, which may be a complete or partial, temporary or permanent refusal of child benefits. The measure has to be proportional with the degree of culpability of the person. If there is no culpability at all, no measure is imposed. The measure has to be in accordance with the seriousness of the conduct and the degree of culpability of the insured person. A measure is not applied if a fine is imposed in respect of the same conduct.

Chapter 3. Child Budgets

236. In 2009 the Act on the child budgets (*Kindgebonden budget*) was introduced. These replaced previous tax deductions for children, since low income families did not really benefit from these since they were not or hardly subject to taxes. The child budgets mentioned below are paid if the household income is not more than EUR 19,758 per year, if it is higher the budgets decrease. The child budgets are paid by the Tax Office (the division also dealing with supplements for care, so it has a good overview of the household income).

237. The amounts of the child budgets are as follows in 2017.

Household	*Amount Per Year for a Family*
1 child	EUR 1,142
2 children	EUR 2,092
3 children	EUR 2,275
For the fourth and next child	EUR 2,381 plus EUR 285 extra per year for each child
Supplement for single parent	EUR 3,076 per year

Maximum capital in 2017:

Partner?	*Maximum Capital on 1 January 2017*
Without partner	EUR 107,752
With partner	EUR 132,752

Partners are those that count for calculating subsistence benefit, i.e., everyone with whom one is sharing a household, that may also be an adult child or a parent.

If the child is between 12 and 18 years of age, the budget per child is increased by the following amounts: 12–15 years old: EUR 233 and 16 and 17 years old: EUR 415.

Part V. Incapacity for Work

Chapter 1. Introduction

238. The first Act providing disability benefits came into force in 1901. This was the *Ongevallenwet* (Industrial Accidents Act), which offered factory workers protection for the financial consequences of industrial accidents in the form of a compulsory insurance scheme. They could claim a benefit that was related to their last earned income. In 1921 occupational diseases were put on a par with industrial accidents. Separate Acts were created to compensate those who suffered accidents at sea, in agriculture and in horticulture. In addition, compulsory insurance schemes were established for employees who had become incapacitated because of a reason other than an industrial accident or an occupational disease (*see* paragraphs 287 et seq.).

239. Introduced in the 1920s, the ZW provided a benefit for temporary incapacity, which was related to the most recent wage of the claimant. Sickness benefits could be claimed for a maximum period of six months. Persons with permanent invalidity could claim an invalidity pension under the *Invaliditeitswet* (Invalidity Act). Persons with a temporary invalidity that had lasted for more than six months were also eligible for a pension. The level of this pension depended, among other things, on the amount of contributions paid and the terms of the insurance. Benefits to disabled miners were regulated in a separate Act.

240. This system of disability insurance schemes for the private sector came under heavy criticism after the Second World War. In particular, the differences in entitlement depending upon whether the person had become incapacitated as a result of an industrial accident/occupational disease or not became increasingly a matter of discussion. Finally this led to the adoption of the WAO. The Industrial Accidents and Invalidity Acts were repealed and radical changes were made to the ZW. The legislature's starting point for the revision of the disability insurance system was that it did not matter any longer why a person had become incapacitated. Instead, the fact that he was incapacitated was important. Until 2004, claimants became entitled to disability benefits after a waiting period of fifty-two weeks.

Although since 1967 drastic changes have repeatedly been made to the system of income protection in case of incapacity to work, the distinction between short- and long-term incapacity has always remained a central element of the system. This central element is also expressed in the setup of the following chapters.

241. The regulations offering income protection in case of short-term incapacity are discussed in Chapter 1. Chapter 2 deals with the regulations providing financial security in case of long-term incapacity. Both chapters deal with incapacity to work as a result of illness or infirmity. Income protection in case of incapacity to work as a result of pregnancy or childbirth is discussed in Chapter 3. Measures aimed at the reintegration into employment of the disabled are only indirectly dealt with in this part. These measures are discussed in Part IX (paragraphs 529 et seq.). As mentioned above, the regulations supplementing the income of incapacitated persons to the social minimum are not discussed in this part, but in Part X (paragraphs 543 et seq.).

Chapter 2. Sickness

242. The income protection for employees during the initial period of incapacity for work has undergone several major changes over the past few years. Up to 1 January 1994, employees could claim sickness benefit amounting to 70% of their wages under the ZW during the first fifty-two weeks of their incapacity to work. A statutory change that was made on 1 January 1994 considerably diminished the relevance of this Act. From that moment on, sickness benefit was paid only after a period of six weeks had elapsed. For employees working for employers with fewer than fifteen employees, the waiting period was only two weeks. In order to prevent employees from being without income during the first six (or two) weeks of their sick leave, the BW provided that the employer was obliged to pay 70% of the wage sum to his employee during this period (sick pay).

243. As of 1 March 1996, an employer has to pay 70% of the wages to an ill employee during a period of fifty-two weeks, as is provided by the BW. In turn, the ZW provides that an employee who can claim sick pay from his employer does not receive sickness benefits on the basis of this Act. The rationale for shifting the responsibility for the income provision of ill employees to employers is that, as a result of the financial effects, employers are expected to check more carefully whether an employee is rightfully absent or not. Employers can take out private insurance to cover their risk, or they can bear it themselves.

The ZW serves as a safety net provision only. This is the case if the employment is terminated during the fifty-two-week period; in this case the employee may claim sickness benefit amounting to 70% of his wages for the remainder of that period. The ZW is also essential for several categories of persons who are not employees in the sense of the BW but who are covered by the ZW. Examples are persons who have been put on a par with employees, such as homeworkers. WW recipients may also claim benefits under the ZW in case of incapacity to work. Also in some specific circumstances, benefits under the ZW are payable, including the case of persons who were recently in receipt of disability benefit and employed again and persons who donated organs. In the *Wet arbeid en zorg* (Act on Work and Care), special rules are made for pregnant women and young mothers.

As of 2006, the maximum period of sick pay is even 104 weeks.

244. This chapter will first pay attention to the private law regulations with regard to sick pay in Articles 7:629 et seq. of the BW (section 1). The ZW will be discussed in section 2.

§1. Sick Pay

I. Field of Application

245. The provision on sick pay of Article 7:629 of the BW applies to employees, that is to say to those who have concluded a contract of employment with an employer as referred to in Article 7:610 of that Code. An agreement is only considered as a contract of employment if three conditions have been met. In the first place, the employee must have committed himself to do work in person (he cannot have himself replaced by another without the employer's consent). In addition, the employer must have committed himself to pay wages to the employee in exchange for this work. A third requirement is that the employee does the work under supervision of the employer. This third requirement is usually satisfied if the employer has the power to give the employee instructions with regard to the work to be done and if the employee is obliged to comply with these instructions (paragraphs 111 et seq.).

246. The provision of Article 7:629 of the BW applies to all employees. No distinction is made between manual and white-collar workers; between old and young employees; between fixed-term and permanently employed persons; between part-timers and full-timers; or between employees who are employed in the Netherlands and those who work abroad. There is one exception to this rule. This exception concerns employees who, as a rule, work for a private employer for less than four days a week performing household tasks, caring for children or providing personal care or nursing. In case of sickness, they can only claim sick pay for a period of six weeks. For the other employees, the period is 104 weeks. The rules for household workers are severely criticized by some pressure groups for affecting mainly women negatively, but so far without result.

II. Conditions

247. In accordance with Article 7:629 of the BW, the employee maintains the right to wages 'if he has not done the agreed work on the grounds that he was unable to do so because of illness'. In the following paragraphs, attention will be paid to the various elements of the quoted definition of the incapacity concept (section A). In some situations there is no entitlement to sick pay. These exclusion grounds will be discussed in section B.

A. Incapacity to Work

248. The definition given above shows that 'illness' must be the cause of the inability to work. Although it is not said in so many words, 'infirmity' will have to be regarded as illness in relation to the sick pay regulation. The concepts of illness and infirmity have the same meaning as in the ZW (paragraph 271). Other causes that prevent the agreed labour from being carried out, such as insufficient training or experience, slight build, advanced age or a maladjusted disposition, do not offer the employee the possibility to claim sick pay under Article 7:629 of the BW.

249. In order to be entitled to sick pay, illness or infirmity must lead to an 'inability to work'. This means that the employee is not only prevented from carrying out work if he is *unable* to carry out the work agreed on, but also if he is *not allowed* to carry out that work if this may have such a damaging effect on his health or that of others that it is irresponsible or cannot, in all fairness, be demanded. This may be the case if an employee has become overwrought as a result of a labour conflict and if, upon his recovery, he should again have to cease work owing to a tense working environment. The employee's own view that he cannot or may not work is insufficient to assume an inability to work, at least if this impression is not substantiated by medical findings. This is not different if the employee feels he is incapacitated to work on the basis of recommendations (which later on proved to be wrong) by his GP or the specialist in attendance.

250. In order to maintain the right to wages, the employee must be prevented from carrying out the work he agreed to do (in his contract of employment). By this term is meant the work the employer and employee have agreed that the employee will perform. In the contract of employment, the work agreed upon may be defined in broad terms. It may happen that an employee, due to illness or infirmity, is unable to do the work he has recently been doing but he may still be able to perform other activities belonging to the labour agreed on. In that case, the employee is not incapacitated for work in the sense of Article 7:629 BW. In this respect there is a distinction between the incapacity to work concept discussed here and that of the ZW. The concept of incapacity to work of the ZW concerns the work that the person in question has recently and factually been doing before he had to stop working due to illness or infirmity (paragraph 273).

B. Grounds for Exclusion

251. In some situations there is no entitlement to sick pay. This is, first of all, the case if the employee has deliberately caused his illness. Deliberately causing illness is very rarely found by the courts, since irresponsible behaviour is not sufficient for assuming this (e.g., drinking too much alcohol), instead the person must deliberately have aimed at hurting himself.

Entitlement to sick pay does not exist if the illness is the result of a disability about which the employee has given false information at the time of the interview procedure. Such medical examination is, however, allowed only in specific circumstances, i.e., if the job concerned requires a specific medical condition.

There also is no entitlement to sick pay for the period in which the employee purposely hinders or delays his recovery. In other words, the employee must contribute to his recovery under penalty of exclusion from his entitlement to sick pay.

Furthermore, entitlement to sick pay does not exist for the period during which an employee does not carry out suitable work for his employer without sound reasons, although he is capable to do so and the employer enables him to do so. The employer can also have the incapacitated person do suitable work for a third party instead of the labour agreed on. If the employee refuses to do so without sound reasons, there is no entitlement to sick pay.

252. The employee only has a right to sick pay if he would have been entitled to wages had he not become incapacitated. Subsequently, an employee is not entitled to wages if he becomes ill while participating in a strike, during the period he is in prison or during a period of unpaid leave.

III. Level and Duration of Sick Pay

253. The main rule is that the employee maintains the right to 70% of his wages for a period of 104 weeks. This period starts on the first day of the employee's incapacity to work, i.e., the first day on which the employee has not worked due to illness or infirmity or on which he has ceased work during working hours owing to the same reasons. If the employee resumes his work and becomes incapacitated again *within* a period of four weeks, he is entitled to the remainder of 104 weeks. In other words, no new period of 104 weeks starts. If the interruption is more than four weeks, a new period of 104 weeks starts. After these 104 weeks, when the employee has been doing suitable work, he is not entitled to sick pay, when he falls ill again. However, if his contract has been changed and his new work has become his agreed work, he is entitled to sick pay in a new case of sickness. The change of the contract can, however, most times not be tacitly assumed; it has to be explicitly agreed on. In the situation that there is no right to sick pay anymore, there is no right to sickness benefit either, as decided by the CRvB (28 juli 2010, ECLI:NL:CRVB:2010:BN2809).

254. There are exceptions to the rule that, in case of incapacity to work, the employee maintains the right to wages during 104 weeks. This period is longer if the employer is late in informing the Uwv of the fact that the employee has become incapacitated. On the basis of Article 38 of the ZW, this notification should take place thirteen weeks after the first day of the incapacity. The period of 104 weeks is extended by the duration of the delay in the notification of the incapacity. A second exception concerns the period of continued pay to employees who perform household work for a private person during less than four days a week. These employees receive continued pay not over a period of 104 weeks, but only six weeks.

255. The right to sick pay is connected to the existence of the contract of employment. If the contract of employment is terminated before the end of the 104 week period, the right to sick pay is also terminated. However, the employer is not supposed to unilaterally escape his obligation to pay sick pay by terminating the contract of employment. First of all, under dismissal protection law, ill employees can be given notice in exceptional cases only. If the employer still dismisses an employee and the employee agrees with this, his ZW benefit may be refused completely in this case. Also, the right to unemployment benefit may be barred.

256. No deviation from the statutory right to sick pay is allowed, if this is disadvantageous to the employee. There is only one exception to this rule. Employer and employee may agree that the employee is not entitled to wages during the first two days of his incapacity.

257. As described above, the BW does not prescribe that the employee continues to receive the full wage in case of incapacity. Instead, he is entitled to 70% of his wage. Employers are allowed to pay more, though. The statutory right to sick pay has a minimum and a maximum level. The minimum threshold is 100% of the applicable statutory minimum wage (EUR 70.95 per day, twenty days per months) during the first fifty-two weeks. The statutory ceiling for the employer's liability is 70% of the maximum basis for the calculation of the sickness benefit (i.e., EUR 202 per day in 201), but, as was said, the employer may be required to pay more on the basis of contractual rules (*see* paragraph 280).

258. In order to prevent undesirable overlapping of entitlements, it has been decided that the wages to which the employee is entitled is reduced if certain types of income are received.

One such type is benefits which the employee receives in connection with his illness in accordance with a compulsory insurance (for instance, ZW benefit, if he donates an organ).

A second form concerns the situation in which the employee, instead of doing the work agreed on which he is unable to do, carries out work which he is able to do for a third party. In this case, 70% of the wages earned with this work is deducted from the sick pay.

259. Employer and employee may always deviate from the statutory rules if it is to the employee's advantage. For instance, they may agree that in case of illness the full wage continues to be paid. Many collective agreements indeed require payment of 100% of the wages. Since the government wishes to give incentives for ill employees to take up work as soon as possible, it encourages social partners to pay not more than 170% over the two-year period. This may mean 100% in the first and 70% in the second year, but 85% and 85% are also options. This approach is not compulsory, as it would infringe on the freedom of negotiation of the social partners.

The approach of pay lower sick pay in the second year was realized for those on a minimum income: the threshold of 100% of the minimum wage applies for the first fifty-two weeks of sickness only.

IV. Obligations and Grounds for Exclusion

260. The following obligations are relevant to the statutory sick pay, and exclusion from sick pay is limited to situations where these obligations are not satisfied. For the non-statutory part (based on collective labour agreements) also other grounds for refusing payment of sick pay may apply, for instance if an employee does not refrain from dangerous sports after having been warned to do so.

The first ground of exclusion is that an employee deliberately caused his illness. Moreover, the employee has to cooperate in realizing his recovery.

In addition, the employee is obliged to do suitable work if he is capable of doing so and given the opportunity by the employer to do this work. The employer may even have the employee do suitable work for a third party. If the employee refuses to do suitable work he loses the right to sick pay completely, even if, for instance, it is a part-time job he refuses whereas he worked full-time before (Hoge Raad 6 juni 2014, ECLI:NL:HR:2014:1341).

261. Violation of these obligations is punishable by exclusion of the right to sick pay (*see* paragraph 249). Reasonableness and fairness may limit the exclusion of sick pay. According to standards of reasonableness and fairness, it is unacceptable, for instance, that the employer completely terminates sick pay in case of a minor offence by the employee.

262. The employer needs information in order to be able to ascertain whether the employee is entitled to sick pay. The employer can instruct the employee with regard to supplying the information he needs in this connection. These instructions have to be in writing, and they must be reasonable. As long as the employee does not comply with such verification rules, the employer has the power to suspend payment of wages.

V. Disputes

263. The employer has to inform the employee if the employer suspects the following:

- an employee who has been reported ill is not really incapacitated (paragraphs 246 et seq.);
- the employee does not observe the verification regulations (paragraph 260); or
- the employee receives benefits or income which are deductible (paragraph 256).

An employer cannot use one of these reasons for a total or partial termination or a suspension of sick pay if he has not informed the employee without delay. The legislator has made this rule to prevent the employee from being confronted with a refusal by the employer to pay sick pay at such a late stage that it is almost impossible for him to prove that he was indeed entitled to sick pay (Article 7:629(7) BW).

264. If a dispute before court relates to the incapacity to work, an expert report is required in order for the claim to be admissible for the court. This report is in principle to be demanded from the Uwv, but a collective agreement can identify other institutions as expert in this matter. The assessment for the report has to be done impartially and to the best of the expert's ability. If the expert is a doctor, he is authorized to get the relevant information on the employee from the physicians in attendance. These physicians are obliged to supply the information requested insofar as this is not too damaging to the employee's privacy (Article 7629(a)(4) BW).

The judge is not bound by the report. At the request of the employer, the employee or, by virtue of his office, the judge, may order the expert to explain or supplement his statement verbally or in writing. In deviation from the rules which apply in other civil law proceedings, an employee can only be ordered to pay the legal cost in case of evidently unreasonable use of procedural law.

VI. Recovery of Damages by the Employer

265. The employee's incapacity to work may be caused by an event for which a third party is obliged to compensate the employee under civil law. In this connection, Article 6:107a BWBW first of all provides that the judge, when determining the compensation under civil law, take into account any wage claims the employee may make in case of incapacity to work on account of Article 7:629 BW or on account of the individual or collective labour agreement. In other words, the employee's compensation claim is limited to the amount of the damage which exceeds his continued pay of wages claims. This is referred to as the residual claim. Second, Article 6:107a of the BW stipulates that the employer who is obliged to continue to pay wages to the employee during his incapacity to work may recover the amount paid in wages from the person who, under civil law, is obliged to compensate him. The amount of the employer's claim is maximized. This maximum is formed by the amount for which the liable person would be liable should no continued obligation to pay wages exist, less the amount of the previously mentioned residual claim. The employer cannot recover losses if the liable person is one of his other employees, except in the case where that other employee has deliberately or consciously acted in a reckless manner.

VII. Extension of the Sick Pay Period

266. In paragraph 252 we discussed that an incapacitated employee can claim continued sick pay after the period of 104 weeks if the employer is late in notifying the Uwv of the employee's incapacity to work. The period that the employer is obliged to continue to pay wages is extended by the period of delay in reporting the employee sick. No disability benefit is paid during the extended period of continued pay of wages (Article 43(b)).

Moreover, the period of sick pay can be extended by a maximum period of one year by the Uwv if the employer has taken insufficient steps to have the employee reintegrated into work. During this period of extension of the obligation to pay wages, no WIA benefit is paid. This was the effect of the *Wet Verbetering Poortwachter* (Law on Improving the Gatekeeper) which introduced the rules to reinforce the maintenance of the duties to help the employee return to work. In order to be eligible for a WIA benefit, a reintegration report has to be reproduced. This report must show the activities of the employer and employee undertaken for the purpose of reintegration of the latter into work. In regulations it is defined which activities have to be undertaken during the first two years of incapacity for work (i.e., the waiting period for WIA benefit). If the employer and employee do not satisfy their duties, the claim for the WIA benefit is not dealt with by the Uwv for a maximum period of one year. During this postponement, the employer has to continue to pay wages. If the employee refuses to cooperate in the reintegration activities, the employer can suspend the payment of wages. In such a case, the employer and/or employee can ask for a report from the Uwv if they disagree on which work is suitable.

VIII. The Obligations of the Employer and Employee for Reintegration of the Sick Employee

267. Although the obligation of the employer to continue to pay wages should encourage him to do his utmost to get the sick employee back into work, this is not automatically the case. It can happen that a private insurance covers all costs for the employer or that an employee is only able to cooperate in reintegration after eighteen months (for instance, after a very serious accident), and the employer then considers the costs of reintegration too high in relation to possible savings in case of reintegration (the employee can be dismissed after two years of illness).

For this reason, the Dutch legislator introduced additional legislation to oblige employers and employees to undertake reintegration efforts. On the basis of this legislation, employers and employees are required to undertake reintegration initiatives if it is expected that sickness will last for a certain period and the employee will not be able to do his/her own work again. At the beginning of the sickness period the employee is assessed by a medical doctor, who has to inform the employer on the possibilities for this employee. This must be done without telling the employer the medical details, since the privacy of the employee must not be infringed.

If an employee is expected to be ill for more than six weeks, the employer and employee are obliged to make a plan for reintegration. In the plan it can be provided, for instance, that the workplace of the employee is adjusted and/or that training for another job or work experience in another job have to be tried. The employer and employee have to meet on a regular basis to see how the reintegration efforts proceed and if the plan has to be adjusted.

The Civil Code was amended in order to explicitly lay down the obligations of the employer and employee. Parties can now require, if necessary also in court, the other to cooperate.

The idea underlying this approach is that the longer the inactivity of the employee lasts, the more difficult it becomes to reintegrate and, without further measures, s/he is on the road to full disability. It is therefore important that, from the earliest possible stage, the employer and employee closely cooperate to implement reintegration measures.

The assessment of these reintegration activities takes place at the moment of the claim for disability benefit, i.e., after 104 weeks of sickness. When, after this period has expired, the employee, in spite of the reintegration efforts, has to claim disability benefit, s/he has to produce a report on the reintegration activities which have taken place. If the employer's actions are considered insufficient by the benefit administration, the employer has to continue to pay wages for another period (for a maximum of twelve months). If it is the employee who has not cooperated satisfactorily, he can be refused disability benefit for a certain period. The system described here was introduced by the so-called *Wet Verbetering Poortwachter* (Gatekeepers Act), narrowing the gate to the WIA.

§2. The Ziektewet

I. Field of Application

A. Who Is Insured under the ZW?

268. As we have already seen in the previous section, not every insured person will receive sickness benefit in case of incapacity to work. With a few exceptions (Article 29(2) ZW under e and f, *see* paragraph 271), no sickness benefit is paid to an insured person who, on account of an employment relationship, is entitled to wages as referred to in Article 7:629 BW (paragraphs 243 et seq.). The main rule, therefore, is that the person who can claim wages from his employer is not entitled to sickness benefit. The ZW is meant as a safety net for specified groups only.

269. The ZW insures employees. Under this Act, employees are those who have concluded a contract of employment with an employer, as referred to in Article 7:610 of the BW. Various types of labour relations have been put on a par with a labour agreement, subject to certain conditions. People reaching the age of 65 are no longer employees. *See* paragraphs 108 et seq. for further information on this subject.

Various categories of persons who do not work but receive a benefit are considered as employees under the ZW. This particularly concerns people who receive a benefit on account of the statutory sickness benefits, disability and unemployment insurance schemes.

270. Although the insured have a right to sickness benefit in case of sickness benefit, it is not paid if they have an employer. This is also the case even if the employer pays no or less wages than due because he and the employee have agreed on waiting days (paragraph 254); because the employee is excluded from the right to continued payment of wages (paragraph 249); or because the employee receives benefits or income which have been deducted from the wages (paragraph 256). The same applies if payment of wages has been suspended because the employee does not observe the verification rules (paragraph 259). This has been regulated in Article 29(1) ZW.

B. Who May Receive Sickness Benefit?

271. Article 29(2) ZW enumerates the categories of persons who receive sickness benefit in case of incapacity to work:

(a) The first category includes persons who are not working on the basis of a contract of employment as meant in Article 7:610 of the BW, but whose labour relation is assimilated with such a contract for the ZW. In other words, these are persons who are not employees for the BW, but they are so for the ZW. These persons do not have an employer from whom, in case of incapacity, they can claim sick pay on account of Article 7:629 BW.
(b) The second category consists of persons who become incapacitated shortly after the insurance under the ZW has expired. These persons do not have an employer either to whom they can turn for income protection in case of short-term incapacity to work. If a person has been continually insured for every day during a period of two months before the insurance has elapsed, the incapacity has to start within one month after the insurance has ended. This term is eight days instead of one month if the person in question was insured for at least sixteen days during the course of the two months preceding the end of the insurance.
(c) The right to sick pay depends on the continuation of the contract of employment. If the contract of employment is terminated before the 104 week period has lapsed, the right to sick pay also ceases to exist. The incapacitated person is entitled to ZW benefits for income protection for the remainder of the 104 week period.
(d) Those who receive WW (unemployment) benefit are insured under the ZW. They do not have an employer who, in case of incapacity, has to continue to pay wages on account of Article 7:629 of the BW. This is why they receive sickness benefit.

(e) Sickness benefit on the basis of ZW is also paid to insured persons who are incapacitated as a result of organ donation. The sickness benefit is deducted from the wages payable by the employer (paragraph 256). As a result, sick pay due by the employer is reduced to nil. This is also the case if employer and employee have agreed that in case of incapacity not 70% but, for instance, 100% of the wage will be paid. This is because the sickness benefit in case of incapacity as a result of organ donation is 100% and not 70% of the daily wage (paragraphs 279 et seq.). In this way, an impediment is removed with regard to the donation of organs by employees.

(f) The last category of persons receiving ZW benefits consists of employees who were disabled immediately preceding their employment. If, in case of incapacity, these employees can claim sick pay, they are entitled to sickness benefit over periods of sick leave during a five-year period upon the start of employment. Since the sickness benefit is deducted from the wage (paragraph 256), the sick pay due by the employer is reduced to practically nil. This also applies when employer and employee have agreed that, in case of incapacity, not 70% but, for instance, 100% of the wage should be paid. At the employer's request, the sickness benefit will be increased to a maximum of 100% of the daily wage (paragraph 279). With this rule, the legislator intends to stimulate employers to employ disabled persons. It is hoped that employers will put aside their concern that the absenteeism rate is higher among disabled employees than among employees who are not disabled.

Some 75% of the beneficiaries are temporary agency workers, persons whose contract of employment has expired or unemployed persons.

II. Conditions

272. A condition for the entitlement to sickness benefit is that the claimant is incapable of doing his work as a direct and objective medically determined consequence of illness. Infirmity is also considered an illness (Article 19 ZW). The incapacity to work concept of the ZW is often described in case law as not being able or allowed to do suitable work on medical grounds and according to objective standards.

A. Incapacity to Work

273. The 'illness' and 'infirmity' concepts have not been defined in the law. Illness denotes a process-wise event consisting of a disruption of physical or mental functions of a human being accompanied by a decrease in the level of power of performance. Such a disruption may stop after a longer or shorter period as a result of the fact that health has been restored to its original level. It is also possible that a new balance is found at another (or in other words, diminished) level of health. In the latter case, it may be said that the illness has led to infirmity. By infirmity we do not mean only acquired disabilities but also congenital ones. With regard to the meaning of the infirmity concept, the case law frequently seeks alliance with common usage. The case law further shows that a person who is not able to do his work owing to a lack of education or experience is not incapacitated as a result of illness or infirmity.

Limitations in connection with low intelligence, slight build, advanced age or maladjusted disposition of an insured person are not considered as illness or infirmity either. Illness and infirmity together may be described as objective deviations of that which is deemed normal in physical or mental respect. Such a description first of all assumes that the medical science is capable of indicating when the human body and mind are functioning normally and when they are not. In particular, the boundary between normal and abnormal with respect to the psyche is difficult to define in practice. Second, the description indicates that the deviation from the standard has to be objectified. The idea behind this is that if doctors cannot find an objective reason for pain symptoms expressed by the insured person, there will probably be no illness or infirmity. Under very special circumstances, the benefit administration (and the judge) will, however, give the insured person the benefit of the doubt. In such cases, the opinion of the consulted physicians as to the reality of his symptoms is essential.

274. Illness or infirmity is relevant only if it leads to 'incapacity to work'. Incapacity to work denotes a situation in which the level of someone's power of performance is insufficient in view of his work requirements. Insufficient does not only mean that the person in question is incapable of doing his work. It is also insufficient if the insured person is not allowed to do his work because this will have such damaging effects on his health or that of others that working is deemed irresponsible or that it cannot, in all fairness, be demanded. The subjective impression of the insured person that he cannot work or is not allowed to work is insufficient ground to assume incapacity to work if, at any rate, this impression is not supported by the eventual medical findings. This is not otherwise if the insured person is of the opinion that he is incapacitated from work on the basis of recommendations later proven wrong made by his family doctor or specialist in attendance. The sector in question has no competence in assessing whether an entitlement to sickness benefit exists.

275. The fact that an insured person is incapacitated from work has to be assessed on the basis of 'his work'. In general, as his work is considered the work that the insured person last – before ceasing that work due to illness or infirmity – and on fact did. The work agreed on by contract by the insured person and his employer or the work that would be done after the insured person had been declared healthy is, therefore, not relevant. When the insured person becomes ill during a period that he receives unemployment benefit, the last work he did before the start of the unemployment period must be the basis for the assessment of his incapacity to work. The situation is different if the employee becomes eligible for unemployment benefit after he has received sickness benefit for the maximum duration of the benefit and has remained permanently incapacitated to do his former work. If he should report ill after a while, his incapacity to work is assessed on the basis of work he is ordered to do in all fairness.

276. For those who have been ill for fifty-two weeks a more strict concept applies; this was introduced in 2014 since it was found that sickness beneficiaries had considerably more problems to re-enter work than persons receiving sick pay. This applies only for ZW beneficiaries, but for the fifty-two weeks period also periods count during which the employer has paid sick pay. The criterion now is whether the person can *with generally accepted work* earn only less than 65% of his former wage. This concept of generally accepted work is also used in the WIA. So no longer suitable work is applied as the method to calculate the income but the much broader term of generally accepted work. The assessment of whether a person can still earn this work is done according to the methods used for WIA (*see* the next chapter). So if he person can earn more than 35% of his former wage he is not entitled to sickness benefit anymore and benefit is terminated after one month. The person can then attempt to qualify for unemployment benefit.

B. Grounds for Exclusion

277. The right to sickness benefit is excluded during the period that the insured person lives abroad or stays abroad for more than three months (Article 19(a) ZW). For the calculation of the duration of sickness benefit (paragraphs 277 et seq.), it must be assumed that during the period that there was no right to sickness benefit because this ground of exclusion applies, this benefit was nevertheless paid. The exclusion ground does not apply to insured persons who are living abroad but who are staying in the Netherlands during a continuous period of three months. Nor does it apply when the person concerned lives in a country with which the Netherlands made an international agreement on the basis of which there is a right to sickness benefit.

III. Level and Duration of Sickness Benefit

278. Recipients of sickness benefit are sometimes entitled to a supplement to this benefit by virtue of the Supplementary Benefits Act (TW). The main condition for entitlement to a supplementary benefit under the TW is that the income of the person in question (plus that of his partner, if any) is less than the relevant social minimum (paragraphs 546 et seq.).

A. Duration of Sickness Benefit

279. The first day of sickness benefit payment is not the same for each category of persons. Some receive sickness benefit as of the third day of the incapacity to work. These are people who are not working on the basis of a contract of employment as meant in Article 7:610 of the BW but whose labour relation is assimilated with this for the purpose of insurance under the ZW (paragraph 269 under a). Two waiting days also apply to those who become incapacitated shortly after the termination of the insurance (paragraph 269 under b). People whose employment is terminated within 104 weeks after the beginning of the incapacity receive sickness benefit as of the first day of the incapacity to work after the termination of employment, but not before the third day of the incapacity to work (paragraph 269 under c). Those who become ill while receiving a benefit on account of the WW receive sickness benefit as from the first day of the incapacity to work. There are no waiting days either for people who are incapable of doing their work as a result of organ donation and for employees who are disabled when entering into employment (paragraph 269 under d, e and f).

280. After the first day of eligibility, sickness benefit is paid for every day of the incapacity to work (with the exception of Saturdays and Sundays). The sickness benefit is terminated as soon as the insured person has recovered. The sickness benefit is also terminated as soon as the person in question has been incapacitated for 104 weeks. In order to determine the 104 week term, periods of incapacity to work which succeed each other with an interruption of less than four weeks are accumulated. The sickness benefit is also terminated on the last day of the month preceding the one in which the person in question reaches the age of 65.

B. Level of Sickness Benefit

281. The sickness benefit generally amounts to 70% of the daily wage. Persons who are incapacitated to work as a result of organ donation receive a sickness benefit amounting to 100% of the daily wage (paragraph 269 under e). The sickness benefit for employees who were disabled at the time they entered into employment is raised to a maximum of 100% of the daily wage at the request of the employer (paragraph 269 under f).

282. The basis for the calculation of the sickness benefit is the daily wage. Article 15 of the ZW defines the daily wage as the wage that the insured person could have earned per day in his most recent job if he had not become incapacitated. Further regulations with regard to the daily wage have been laid down by the Minister of Social Affairs and Employment. These regulations define, among other things, which wage elements are taken into account in relation to the calculation of the daily wage and in which way the daily wage should be calculated. The Uwv may set further rules with regard to determining the daily wage for one or more categories of employees.

The daily wage is maximized (Article 17 Wet FSV). This maximum amount is EUR 206.54 a day (2017) – a month has twenty-one days. The maximum benefit is 70% of this amount.

283. The ZW has several provisions on overlapping. One of these prevents the undesirable accumulation of sickness benefit and income from work (e.g., wage from employment or business profit). This is relevant in a situation in which an employee is incapacitated to do 'his work' (paragraph 273), but he is able to do part of his work or other lighter work. The insured person does not receive more sickness benefit than the amount with which his daily wage exceeds his earnings. In addition, there is a statutory rule to prevent overlapping of sickness benefits and benefits in connection with long-term incapacity to work or early retirement or old-age pension.

284. Now that the income protection for ill employees was not guaranteed, in the first place, by the SBA, but also by the statutory obligation of the employer to continue to pay wages, the question arose as to whether this was consistent with international social security conventions.

The Committee of Experts supervising the European Social Charter concluded in its 1995/96 Report[14] that the Dutch system was contrary to Article 12 of the Charter, which obliges states to gradually raise the level of social security. The Committee considered that the scheme infringed the solidarity idea, which can, in the view of the

14. Committee of Experts on the European Social Charter, *Conclusions XIV-1 (1/95-12/96)* (Strasbourg: Council of Europe, 1996).

Committee, be served best by a system funded from contributions or taxes, since this leads to a form of redistribution of the risks. The Dutch Government did not agree with this view and strongly defended the privatized sick pay system which was needed in order to lower the relatively high level of sickness in the Netherlands. Since then the Committee continued to follow the developments closely, in order to be informed of any gaps in the protection of the workers concerned.

285. The ILO Committee of Experts seemed to be less opposed to this form of privatization. The view of the Committee can best be seen in its conclusions concerning the privatization of the SBA in its 73rd Session (2002). It considered that the reform was undertaken to encourage employers to prevent and reduce employee absenteeism due to sickness, which was much higher in the Netherlands than in other, comparable countries. The Dutch government expected that market forces and competition would prove to be more effective in achieving this goal. At the same time, the government took care to maintain the basic social security benefits provided under the SBA in all cases in which employers and market forces failed to produce the desired effect. Moreover, the Committee considered that a number of additional legislative measures safeguarded entitlements of the persons protected. These were gradually put in place to mitigate the negative effects of the market forces, which tend to discriminate against the weak and vulnerable and undermine the basic spirit of solidarity inherent in any social security system. The Committee concluded that it 'is bound to observe' that the resulting reforms of the sickness and disability benefits schemes are intended to harness the positive effects of privatization and market forces. As the same time, their negative effects are contained within the basic social security framework. This system has no comparison in the history of social security in Europe. It is thus only natural, the Committee continued its observations, that the reforms pose many new problems of organization and governance of such mixed social security systems. This is particularly true during the transition period. During this period, new forms of state supervision of the system, the democratic participation of the persons protected in its management, the redistribution of risk, financial burden and responsibility in society, and the principles of non-discrimination and solidarity with the most vulnerable groups are consolidated. The Committee concluded that while there is no single right model of social security, all systems should conform to certain basic principles of good governance and social cohesion. The observance of these requirements comes under the general responsibility of the state established in Articles 71(3) and 72(2) of Convention 102.

286. On basis of the circumstance that the Dutch privatized sick pay scheme is a comprehensive system with safety nets, the Committee did not come to a final conclusion that the scheme is contrary to Convention 102. However, it clearly wants to supervise it closely, in order to be informed of possible problems.

Chapter 3. Long-Term Incapacity to Work

§1. Introduction

287. Chapter 1 of this Part dealt with the way in which income protection in case of short-term incapacity to work is realized. This income protection proved to be mainly solved by rules of private law (for persons who are employed on the basis of a contract of employment). The social insurance against the risk of short-term incapacity to work, the ZW, has a limited scope only.

The legal framework is entirely different for persons whose incapacity to work has lasted for more than 104 weeks. These persons are covered by the WIA.

288. Prior to 1998, there was a national insurance scheme against the financial consequences of long-term incapacity to work in addition to the then disability law for employees (WAO), i.e., the AAW. This Act was particularly important for self-employed persons, students and persons who had become disabled before they turned 18 (and students). They could claim a benefit amounting to 70% of the minimum wage in case of total incapacity to work. The AAW was replaced by the Wajong and *Wet arbeidsongeschiktheidsverzekering zelfstandigen* (WAZ [Invalidity Insurance (Self-Employed Persons) Act]) in 1998, since the AAW was found too generous as it included all residents. Earlier attempts to restrict the personal scope of the Act by requiring a certain income to be earned before the claim was made appeared problematic in view of equal treatment provisions (men and women) of EC law (Directive 79/7) Subsequently the Act was repealed.

289. The WIA is the successor of the WAO and is an employees' benefit scheme. By virtue of this Act, employees receive in case of total and permanent incapacity to work 75% of the previously earned wage (up to the maximum daily wage). In case of a lower incapacity degree the level op benefit is lower.

290. The WAO was replaced by the WIA, since, from the government's perspective, the number of WAO recipients was too high. In December 2003, 786,000 persons received this benefit (whereas the working population at the time was 7.3 million). In view of these high figures, several attempts were made to reduce the influx, and this finally led to a new approach, the WIA.

Some explanations for the high figures are: the lack of requirements on employment record for eligibility; the lack of the relation between employment record and level of benefit; the use of the WAO benefit to mitigate the effects (i.e., mass dismissals) of the restructuring of industry in the 1970s and 1980s; and the lack of sufficient efforts of the benefit administration to get disabled people back into work.

291. The WIA makes a distinction between persons who are permanently and fully incapacitated to work and others. The first category is given a benefit of 75% of the previously earned wage; for the second category the level of benefit depends on whether they are working or not.

292. The WIA solely applies to persons who became disabled after 1 January 2004. Those who were already disabled before this time remain entitled to a WAO benefit. Thus WIA is only for new cases.

293. The WAZ – the self-employed scheme – provided a benefit to self-employed people in case of long-term incapacity to work. In case of total incapacity to work, the level of the benefit amounted to 70% of the profit in the fiscal year or of the average annual profit over the last three tax years before the start of the incapacity, with a maximum of 70% of the statutory minimum wage. The WAZ was an insurance scheme. The benefits were financed from contributions paid by the insured.

The Wajong provides a benefit to people who have become disabled at an early age and to students in case of long-term incapacity to work amounting to 75% of the minimum wage in case of total incapacity. The Wajong is not a social insurance scheme, but a provision. The benefits on account of this Act are financed from general funds.

294. In the following paragraphs of this chapter, we shall discuss the WIA and the Wajong.

§2. The Wet Werk en Inkomen Naar Arbeidsvermogen

I. Structure of the Act

295. A main element of the WIA is the distinction between persons who are at least 80% permanently disabled and others. This distinction is elaborated under the WIA in the *Inkomensvoorziening volledig arbeidsongeschikten* (IVA [Income Provision for the Fully Disabled]) for the first group and the *Werkhervattingsregeling gedeeltelijk arbeidsgeschikten* (WGA [Scheme on the Take-Up of Work by Persons Who Are Partially Able to Work]) for the other. The IVA and WGA may seem two different types of benefit, but they are payable on the basis of the same Act, the WIA.

296. The idea underlying the IVA is that persons who are permanently disabled, and therefore not able to take up work again, should be given a good income provision. The WAO had been changed to such extent in previous years that the income provision on the basis of the law for the fully disabled was found unsatisfactory.

The Scheme on the Take-Up of Work by Persons Who Are Partially Able to Work (WGA) is open for persons who are disabled between 35% and 80%, and also for persons who are disabled for 80% but whose disability is not assessed as permanent. The threshold to the WIA is therefore 35%; this is higher than under the WAO, where it was 15%. WGA refers to its recipients as 'persons who are partially able to work', instead of 'partially disabled', since the focus should be on their ability to work, instead of their inability to work.

WGA recipients receive a wage-related benefit if they satisfy conditions on the employment past; the duration depends on their reemployment past. The rules for entitlement and duration of this benefit follow those of the WW.

After the right to the wage-related benefit has expired, they receive a wage supplement, on condition that they have an income of at least 50% of their earning capacity.

If they do not have an income of at least 50% of their earning capacity, they receive a so-called follow-up benefit.

The wage supplement is relatively generous, whereas the follow-up benefit is very low, as we will *see* below. These rules are meant to encourage to the utmost incapacitated persons to take up work again.

For persons who are disabled less than 35%, there is no income provision on the basis of the WIA. Employers are supposed to keep these persons in work. In case they lose their job, they have to rely on WW benefit or public assistance.

II. Conditions

A. Personal Scope

297. The WIA is an employee scheme. The concept of 'employee' relevant to this Act is similar to that for the ZW (*see also* paragraphs 265 et seq.). Disability benefit is not paid in case of a foreigner who does not stay in the Netherlands legitimately.

B. Incapacity to Work

298. The incapacity concept of the WIA (and previously under the WAO) does not have the same meaning as that of the ZW.

1. Permanently Fully Incapacitated to Work

299. Article 4 WIA defines the term fully and permanently incapacitated to work. An employee is fully and permanently disabled if, as a result of sickness, infirmity, pregnancy or confinement cannot earn more than 20% of his previous earnings per hour. By permanent is meant a medically stable or deteriorating situation. If there is a slight chance of improvement, the person is reassessed yearly during the first five years after he has become entitled to benefit to see whether he is still fully disabled. If he is then still disabled, he will be considered permanently disabled unless there are reasons to assume that he is not permanently disabled.

Also, if a person is able, despite his permanent and full disability, to actually earn more than 20% or more of his previous wage, he will be reassessed, and this may mean a lower benefit or a loss of benefit. There are transitional rules in this case (entitlement to one year of WGA benefit before the termination of benefit rights). If the person earns an income, then 70% of the income is deducted from benefit. About 35% of the WIA benefit recipients receive Iva benefits.

2. Definition of Incapacity for Work

300. The definition of 'incapacity for work' in the WIA requires that there has to be a causal link between reduction of the earning capacity of the claimant and his infirmity or sickness. This causal relationship must be on medical grounds; thus, it has to be assessed by a medical expert. In other words, if a claimant has complaints or restrictions, the doctor has to search for a type of infirmity or sickness which can explain these. If no such infirmity or disease can be found, the claimant is, in principle, not incapacitated for work. As a result, considerable numbers of claims are refused, such as in the case that a person suffers from pains but the cause of which cannot be explained.

The case law on this issue has become a little more relaxed in recent years, since the refusal of benefit in case of obvious complaints, such as heavy pains, was not satisfactory. The present approach is that two or more independent doctors (specialists in attendance do not count) confirm that an applicant has restrictions; incapacity for work may be accepted, provided their view is laid down in a clear, consistent and well-founded way.[15]

301. After the link between medical factors and restrictions has been established, the calculation of the loss or reduction of earning capacity is essential for accepting and calculating incapacity for work.

The remaining earning capacity may be described as the income a person can still earn by working despite his illness or infirmity. For this purpose, all 'generally accepted work which the person in question is able to do with his strength and competence' is taken into account. The income which a healthy person with the capacities of the claimant can earn (the so-called measure man income – most often this is the previously earned income) is compared with the income the claimant can earn in generally accepted work.

The degree of incapacity to work is expressed in a percentage. In order to qualify for benefit, an employee must be at least 35% incapacitated. In order to determine the incapacity percentage, the following formula is used:

Measure man income – remaining earning capacity	x	100%
measure man income		

The outcome is the incapacity rate.

302. Example. A person earned EUR 30 per hour, and his earning capacity is EUR 10. The incapacity rate is calculated as follows:

Measure man income (EUR 30) remaining earning capacity (EUR 10)	100% x	66.6% =
Measure man income (EUR 30)		

The incapacity rate (66.6 in this example) is not the benefit rate. Below we will discuss the relation between incapacity rate and benefit rate.

303. In the following paragraphs, we shall first look at the way in which the level of the measure man income has to be determined. Then we shall focus on the question how the level of the remaining earning capacity has to be determined.

15. CRvB 1 May 1996, *RSV* 1996/161.

3. Measure Man Income

304. First of all it has to be determined whether the claimant is incapacitated at the end of the waiting period. The statutory regulations entail that, once benefit is awarded, the Uwv frequently has to reassess whether the person in question is still incapacitated (paragraph 326). As far as determining the measure man income is concerned, the distinction between the first assessment (paragraphs 298 et seq.) and the subsequent reassessments (paragraph 301) is important.

305. In order to determine the measure man income, the measure man is defined as any person who does the same kind (and the same amount) of work as the person in question did before becoming incapacitated. It could also be said that, in principle, each person is his own measure man, in the following paragraph we will explain why the concept of measure man is still used. The amount that the person in question would have earned himself at the end of the waiting period with the work he most recently did is considered as measure man income. This means that, if an employee used to work part-time, the wage he would have earned at the end of the waiting period by doing this part-time work is considered as measure man income.[16] If the person in question had two jobs, the combination of functions is decisive for the determination of the measure man income.[17] If, in addition to being an employee, he also worked as a self-employed person, only his function as an employee may be considered for the determination of the measure man income.[18]

306. There are exceptions to the principle that each person is his own measure man, that were established in case law. One exception occurs if the claimant had extremely long working days before becoming incapacitated.[19] Adjustment of the measure man income also takes place if the wage the person in question received was much higher than that of other, similar employees working for the same employer.[20] If a person has been unemployed for a considerable period of time when he becomes incapacitated and if he does not receive a benefit related to his latest wage, other activities beside the ones most recently carried out are also considered with regard to the determination of the measure man income. In this case, a measure man is taken to be 'the long-term unemployed person to whom an income amounting to the minimum wage must be attributed'.[21] Deviation from the main rule that each person is his own measure man also takes place if a person is, already at the outset, incapable of doing the work he most recently did as a result of existing limitations. In these cases, the measure man income is determined according to (if possible, previously performed) functions which the person in question *was* capable of performing.[22]

These adjustments explain why the concept of measure man income is used and not always the actually earned income.

16. CRvB 2 Oct. 1978, RSV 1979/10.
17. CRvB 19 Feb. 1971, RSV 1971/175.
18. CRvB 28 Jun. 1974, RSV 1974/445.
19. CRvB 10 Dec. 1971, RSV 1972/77.
20. CRvB 26 Jan. 1982, RSV 1982/165.
21. CRvB 23 Nov. 1993, RSV 1994/85.
22. For instance, CRvB 3 May 1985, RSV 1986/6.

307. As mentioned before, the wage that the person in question would have earned in his own job is (apart from adjustments) considered as measure man income for the determination of the incapacity to work at the end of the waiting period. The words 'would have earned' in the previous sentence indicate that the benefit administration should take into account any changes in the wage level pertaining to the function in question which could reasonably be expected after the person in question ceased his work due to incapacity. The measure man income at the end of the waiting period should present as real an image as possible of the income situation which the person in question would have been in at the time if he had not become incapacitated.

308. Once the measure man income at the end of the waiting period has been determined, any changes occurring in the wage level in the measure function must be disregarded in case of a reassessment. The measure man income is, however, indexed according to the average wage increase in all business sectors in the Netherlands.

309. Changes in the concept of measure man income are not treated in the same way as changes in the concept of measure man. A change in the measure man concept occurs, for instance, in age-bound professions such as professional soccer players and dancers. Even if the person in question had not become incapacitated, in time he would have had to abandon his function and accept a different and, in most cases, a considerably lower paid job. Consequently, a new measure man is determined for the person in question with the corresponding, usually lower, measure man income.[23]

310. The law prescribes that, when determining the degree of incapacity to work, acquired new skills should be taken into account as much as possible for determining the measure man. Acquired new skills may, therefore, lead to a change in the measure man for the person concerned.

As soon as a person qualifies for a new profession, e.g., by means of obtaining a diploma or certificate after he has become incapacitated, a new standard man has to be selected that is in line with the certificate obtained. A change in the measure man on the basis of acquired new skills only takes place, however, if it leads to a higher standard man income.[24] This change in qualification may also lead to a higher earning capacity of the person concerned. In case of a person who is able to work part-time only, for instance the change of the measure person can still lead to a higher benefit.

4. The Calculation of the Residual Earning Capacity

311. The remaining earning capacity may be described as the wage which the claimant can earn by doing 'generally accepted work which he is capable of doing with his strength and competence' in spite of his illness or infirmity. The determination of the earning capacity does not only require a medical assessment (paragraph 305), but also an ergonomic assessment by the job expert working for the Uwv (paragraphs 311 et seq.).

312. A medical expert working for the Uwv, also called an insurance doctor, has to assess whether the claimant suffers from illness or infirmity. It should be remarked that the illness and infirmity concepts are similar to the ones under the ZW (paragraph

23. CRvB 10 Nov. 1992, RSV 1993/131.
24. CRvB 17 Mar. 1981, RSV 1981/181.

271). The insurance doctor must assess to what extent the illness or infirmity of the person concerned lead to limitations with regard to performing work in general.

The insurance doctor has to list the effects of the illness or infirmity for the claimant. As from 1 January 2002, the so-called *Claim Beoordelings-en Borgingssysteem* (CBBS [Claim Assessment and Control System]) is used. This computer system is meant to standardize the practice of assessing claimants and to reduce different outcomes of assessment procedures. In this system, the limitations of claimants to do work are not decisive, but rather their possibilities to work. For the CBBS system, six aspects are relevant: social functioning, adaptation to the environment's requirements, dynamic activities, stationary attitudes, and working times. The first two aspects are mainly meant to assess the possibilities of personals with psychological problems. These aspects concern concentration of attention, ability to show one's feelings, and ability to cope with conflicts and cooperation.

Under the previous system it had to be determined whether the person concerned could reach for 50 centimetres or could walk or sit for a particular period. This system was criticized, as it required hard data which were often difficult to give. In the CBBS system, standard values are given for activities, e.g., the weight of an object which a healthy person of over 16 can carry. These values are illustrated by means of examples from daily life. For instance, where the aspect of carrying is assessed, the following possibilities are given: normal – the person can carry 15 kilograms (pre-school child); slightly limited – he can carry approximately 10 kilograms (such as a toddler); restricted – he can carry approximately 5 kilograms (a bag of potatoes); strongly limited – he can carry approximately 1 kilograms (a litre of milk). The findings are laid down in a list with the possibilities of the claimant and presented to the so-called job expert (*see* paragraph 311 below).

If the limitations are so serious that the person concerned is not able to work at all (e.g., he is fully paralysed), no investigation by the job expert is required. In the view of the legislator, the lack of such an investigation is acceptable in exceptional circumstances only, such as in the case where a person has to lie in bed permanently or constantly needs help with daily general tasks, such as bathing and dressing.

313. At the end of the CBBS procedure, the job expert investigates which types of work the person in question can still do despite his medically indicated limitations. It does not matter in this respect whether the person in question has a real chance of being employed in this work, in other words, whether there are any vacancies. This is because the law explicitly provides that the fact that the person in question can actually obtain the labour should be set aside.

314. The claimant's earning capacity is assessed by determining the 'generally accepted work' he can still do. In other words, not only suitable work, but also all work can be taken into account for this purpose (the work the person did before). Among the jobs the person can do which fit in this concept, the job expert has to choose those in which the claimant will earn the highest wage. The concept of generally accepted work is fairly broad and covers many more types of work than the concept of suitable work. The *Schattingsbesluit* (Assessment decree), a decree that is based on the WIA, gives some further guidance as to which type of work falls within this concept. From this it follows that only few exceptions apply to the work that can be taken into account, an example being jobs which hardly exist in the labour market. An exception also applies if work can only be done by the person in question after changes in the workplace which the employer concerned cannot, in all fairness, be expected to make. If there is a functional age limit for specific work on account of the law or a collective labour agreement, this work may not be used in the case of a person who has already reached that age. Work is not worth considering if the person in question possesses such characteristics that an employer cannot, in all fairness, be expected to employ him for a specific task. This may be the case, for instance, if excessive absenteeism is to be expected.

315. For the selection of jobs relevant to this assessment, the job expert uses the CBBS. This system contains a – non-exhaustive – survey of existing jobs (about 10,000) and indicates what skills (education and experience) are required to hold such a position and what mental or physical requirements the job has. These jobs were selected and analysed in enterprises and this information was inserted in the CBBS. The CBBS furthermore mentions the wages which are paid for the selected jobs.

316. The remaining earning capacity is determined by taking three different job types from CBBS which the claimant can do. A job type is relevant only if it represents at least three jobs in CBBS. For instance, the job type of 'word processor' is relevant only if in the enterprise analysed for CBBS there were three jobs falling within this category. This condition is meant to ensure that only realistic job types are selected to determine the earning capacity. Again it has to be stressed that there need not be actual vacancies in this work.

The job expert has to select those job types which have the highest incomes, as this will lead to higher earning capacity and thus a lower benefit.

The wage of the middle position of the three best paying job types is considered for the determination of the level of the remaining earning capacity.

317. Example. If the person is deemed able to do the work of a telephone operator (EUR 11 per hour), coffee machine repairer (EUR 12) and secretary (EUR 13), the relevant wage is EUR 12.

318. Now that we know the remaining earning capacity, we can compare this with the measure income and thus calculate the incapacity rate according to the formula in paragraph 299.

5. Grounds for Exclusion

319. A ground of exclusion of benefit exists if a person is entitled to sick pay from his employer.

The right to disability benefit is also excluded during the period that the insured person is living abroad or residing there for a period longer than three months. An exception has been made for insured persons who are living abroad but are residing in the Netherlands for a period longer than three months. If a person resides in a country with which a treaty is made which allows export of benefit, the disability benefit is payable.

III. Level and Duration of Disability Benefit

A. The IVA Benefit

320. The IVA benefit is 75% of the monthly wage of the person concerned (up to the maximum monthly wage as determined by the Wet FSV) and is payable until the claimant reaches pension age. If the recipient of IVA benefit has an income from work, 70% of this income is deducted from benefit.

B. The WGA Benefit

321. Persons who are disabled for more than 35% and less than 80%, and also persons who are fully, but not permanently, disabled are eligible for a WGA benefit. In fact the latter group is a large one: in 2014 95,000 persons, whereas 40,000 were partially disabled. Part (around 40%) of the fully but no permanently disabled will later be assessed as permanently fully disabled and then be admitted to IVA.

WGA recipients receive a wage-related benefit if they satisfy conditions on the employment past; the duration depends on their reemployment past. The rules for entitlement and duration of this benefit follow those of the WW.

After the right to the wage-related benefit has expired, they receive a wage supplement, on condition that they have an income of at least 50% of their earning capacity.

If they do not have an income of at least 50% of their earning capacity, they receive a so-called follow-up benefit.

The wage supplement is relatively generous, whereas the follow-up benefit is very low, as we will *see* below. These rules are meant to encourage incapacitated persons to the utmost to resume work.

1. The Wage-Related Benefit

322. The WGA wage-related benefit is 70% of the previous wage (within the limit of the maximum daily wage). For entitlement, it is required that the person satisfies the reference condition, which is the same as for unemployment benefits (*see* paragraphs 422 et seq.). The duration of benefit is related to the duration of the employment (and age) of the claimant.

323. For this purpose, it is required that the claimant have worked in twenty-six weeks out of the last thirty-six weeks before the start of disability (sickness). If this condition is satisfied, the duration of benefit is three months.

324. This period is prolonged if, in each of four calendar years within the five calendar years immediately before the first day of unemployment, the claimant received wages over at least 208 hours a year.

If this condition is satisfied, the (total) benefit period is prolonged by one month for each year that the person received wages over at least 208 hours during the first ten years of work, and after these ten years it is half a month. The maximum is twenty-four months. This rule was introduced in 2016 (and during a transitional period persons still have longer periods, i.e., thirty-eight months was the old maximum period).

325. The employment past is calculated as follows. As from 1998 until 1 January of the year in which a person becomes ill, every year counts in which the person concerned receives wages over at least fifty-two days.

In addition, all years count between the 18th birthday of the claimant and 1998, regardless of the kind of activities (or non-activity) during this period.

Because of the reference to 1998 in the law, the relevance of the fictitious past is gradually decreasing.

326. Example. An employee born 1 August 2000 works from 2016 in a job of forty hours a week. On 1 August 2040 she becomes ill (suppose that the laws remain as they are now). Between 2035 and 1 January 2040, there are four years during which she received wages over at least 208 hours (days in 2040 do not count, as only calendar years before the first day she became ill (entitled to sick pay or sickness benefit) count). The total period is thus twenty-four years and the duration of wage-related benefit is thus seventeen (ten years that lead to one month a year, and fourteen that count as one half) months (that start after the two-year waiting period during which she is paid sick pay).

327. This system was followed as the WGA covers both the disability and unemployment element of a claimant. Under the WAO regime, a partially disabled person could receive both a partial WAO benefit and a partial unemployment benefit. The new system simplifies the rules, but the unemployment benefit approach was followed for calculating the right to and the duration of benefit.

328. If a recipient of WGA benefit receives income from work, 70% of the income is deducted from his benefit.

2. The Wage Supplement Benefit

329. After the right to wage-related benefit has expired, the WGA claimant is entitled to the wage supplement benefit, on condition that he earns income at the level of at least the remaining earning capacity. We discussed the remaining earning capacity in paragraphs 309 et seq. Thus, if a person is supposed to have an earning capacity of EUR 1,000 a month, he must have an income from work of at least 50% in order to be eligible for the wage supplement. The idea lying behind the rule is clear: it must be made as attractive as possible for the person concerned to start working or remain working.

330. The level of the wage supplement is 70% of the difference between the measure man income and the remaining earning capacity. The wage supplement thus does not depend on the income but remains the same regardless of the income earned (up to the amount of the remaining earnings capacity). In other words it is attractive to work as much as possible, since income is not deducted from benefit, except if income is more than the remaining earning capacity. If the income is higher than the remaining earning capacity, 70% of the difference between the monthly wage and the income from work is deducted from benefit.

Suppose the previous wage was 2,100 and the remaining earnings capacity is 1,050. For eligibility of the wage supplement he must actually earn at least 525. The wage supplement is 70% of the previous wage (2,100) minus earnings capacity (1,050), which is 735. Thus if he earns 600, the total income is 1335, and if he earns 800, it is

1,535. If he earns 1200, benefit is 70% (previous age, 2,100 minus the actual income (1,200) = 630, in addition to the income out of work: 1830 is the total income.

331. The wage supplement is payable until the pension age if the person remains disabled. If, however, the income falls below 50% of the remaining earning capacity, the person becomes eligible for the follow-up benefit, *see* below.

3. The Follow-Up Benefit

332. The WGA claimant who, upon expiry of the wage-related benefit, does not satisfy the condition that he earns at least 50% of the remaining earning capacity, is eligible for the follow-up benefit. The level of this benefit is 70% of the statutory minimum wage, or of the actual monthly wage of reference, if lower, in case of full disability. In case of partial disability, the benefit is lower; *see* next paragraph.

333. In case of partial disability the incapacity rate is relevant, as discussed in paragraph 299. This rate follows from the comparison of the measure man income and the remaining earning capacity. The Act mentions five classes (*see* table below in paragraph 334), and the appropriate class is the one in which the incapacity rate fits. With each class, a benefit rate corresponds. This benefit rate has to be applied on the statutory minimum wage. For instance, if a person earned EUR 30 before he became disabled and has a remaining earning capacity of EUR 10, his disability rate is 66.6%, as we saw in paragraph 300. This fits in the class of 65–80, and the benefit rate is thus 50.75%, to be applied on the statutory minimum wage.

334. Table with the classes relevant to the benefit rates.

Incapacity Rate	*Benefit Rate*
35–45	28%
45–55	35%
55–65	42%
65–80	50.75%
80	70%

335. As can be seen, the benefits for partially disabled persons are low and in any case beyond the applicable social minimum (same as minimum wage, in case of a married couple). This means that these persons will have to apply for (means tested) supplements to reach the social minimum (these benefits are discussed in Part X).

IV. Obligations

336. The WIA imposes quite a few obligations on employees. The WGA recipient must inform the Uwv of relevant facts and must cooperate if the Uwv wishes to check the facts.

He is also obliged to prevent having to claim benefit and continuing to claim it insofar as this can reasonably be required of him. For instance, if he undertakes activities which are hazardous to his health, this may affect his benefit entitlement.

The recipient is also obliged to cooperate with his reintegration into work. This may mean that he has to cooperate in medical treatment. It also means that he has to cooperate with reintegration activities, such as training and trial jobs. He is also obliged to do suitable work; these provisions correspond with those of the Unemployment Benefits Act. As we saw above, the WGA incorporates both disability and unemployment benefits, and therefore it is logical that the unemployment benefit rules on accepting suitable work were copied to the WIA.

337. The sanction for violating the general obligation to inform the Uwv of relevant facts is an *administrative fine*. If an employee does not comply with the obligation of attending training, and if he does not observe any of the other obligations, this will lead to an *administrative measure*. This means the total or partial, temporary or permanent refusal of disability benefit.

V. Bearing the Own Risk by Employers

338. During the preparation of the WIA, it was envisaged that it could be administered by private companies. Finally another approach was followed. It was decided that the IVA was to be administered by the Uwv. The WGA is also administered by the Uwv, but employers can opt to accept the risk for WGA benefits. If they choose to do so, they are exempt from contributions for these benefits, but if one of their employees becomes entitled to WGA benefit, the employer has to pay these benefits for a duration of five years. For this purpose, the statutory conditions of the WIA, as discussed above, have to be followed.

339. There are some far-reaching effects of the choice of bearing the risk for WGA benefits. One of these is that the Uwv is not responsible for reintegration efforts for these WGA recipients. The employer has the freedom to expand the reintegration efforts. A second important effect is that in case a WGA recipient does not fulfil his obligations, as discussed in paragraph 335, it is the employer who can impose the measure on the basis of the WIA. The rules of administrative law have to be followed in this case.

§3. Wet werk en arbeidsondersteuning jonggehandicapten

I. Field of Application

340. The Wajong provides for a minimum income provision for persons who were already disabled before the age of 18 or those who became disabled when being a student.[25] This Act was introduced in 1998 (*Stb.* 1997, 177). It then provided for an income provision based on the level of disability (calculated in the same way as for the WAO and WIA), but the percentages following from this were applied on the statutory minimum wage (which is the standard for all minimum income provisions).

25. Act of 3 Dec. 2009, *Stb.* 2009, 580.

341. In the beginning of the twenty-first century, also the Wajong came under discussion as it was found that young people were admitted too easily to the Wajong, without having tried to get them to work. Once they were in the benefit scheme, few initiatives were taken to get them into work. This was found undesirable. It was feared that the number of recipients would continue to grow fast.

342. For this reason in 2010 a new Act was made, the Wet werk en arbeidsondersteuning jonggehandicapten (Wajong). So, like the WIA, this Act has now the term 'work' in its title, to stress that work has priority over income. Those who were already in the 'old' Wajong continue to receive the benefit under the old conditions.

343. The main principle underlying the Act is that also persons with disabilities should have all chances to participate in work, and for this purpose they should also take their chances. For this purpose the capacity of the young disabled is assessed when he applies for benefit. If his restrictions mean that he has, even with support, no chance at all in getting work, he is entitled to benefit at the rate of 75% of the applicable minimum wage (for those under 23 the rates are lower than for persons who are 23 years old and over).

344. If from the assessment it appears that he has chances to find work, he, was, according to the 2010 Act, admitted to the *Werkregeling jonggehandicapten* (Work scheme young disabled). Under the provisions of the scheme the person concerned first had to find work with his own efforts. If this was not successful, he was entitled to support from the Uwv to find work. This support could vary from a work offer to training or guidance in finding or doing work. In this case the income was supplemented in so far the income was lower than the benefit rates.

345. As from 2015 the Wajong is restricted to persons who are fully disabled; for others (newcomers) access will be closed and they have to rely on the *Participatiewet* (Public assistance).

II. Conditions

346. In order to be eligible for the Act a person has to be resident of the Netherlands. Second the person must on his 17th birthday, as a direct result of sickness or infirmity, be unable to earn at least 75% of the statutory minimum wage by working and it must be unlikely that he will recover within a year. The second category is formed by persons who become incapacitated after they have reached the age of 17 and who were students for at least six months in the year which immediately preceded the start of the incapacity. A person is considered to be a student if he is younger than 30 and is engaged in education (receives study grants on basis of the Study Finance Act) or training during the day for an average of 213 clock hours per calendar quarter (Article 5).

The rate of disability is 'finally' determined at the age of 27, or seven years after the start of the benefit, in order to be sure that the person is really disabled. This final determination does not exclude later assessments.

347. The definition of the incapacity to work concept in Article 2:4 of the Wajong is almost identical to the one in the WIA for the IVA. This requires a loss of earning capacity that is a direct consequence of illness or infirmity; the size of the loss of earning capacity is determined by the measure man income and the residual earning capacity (paragraphs 295 et seq.). A difference is that the person concerned must be at least 75% incapacitated in order to be entitled to a benefit. The WIA requires that the incapacity to work must be at least 35%.

348. In a decree, rules may be laid down which deviate from the general rules for determining the degree of incapacity to work if a person may claim benefits on account of more than one regulation covering the financial consequences of long-term incapacity to work. This is the case, for instance, if a person of 16 years of age works in employment becomes incapacitated and is still incapacitated after fifty-two weeks.

The claimant for Wajong benefit is obliged to cooperate in making a work participation plan and has to undergo medical treatment that is adequate according to general medical standards if his contributes to his recovery or maintenance, recovery or improvement of his capacity to work.

349. The entitlement to disability benefit is terminated if the person in question reaches the age of 65, two months after the day he has become able to earn more than 75% of his measure man income, or if he takes up his residence abroad or is imprisoned. If the entitlement to benefit has been terminated as a result of setting up residence abroad and the young disabled person comes back to live in the Netherlands again, the entitlement to benefit revives (Article 2:17).

350. The non-exportability of Wajong is in line with Regulation 883/2004, since Wajong is considered a special non-contributory benefit. Article 3(3) of Regulation 883/2004 provides that the Regulation applies also to the special non-contributory benefits covered by Article 70. Article 70(4) provides that these benefits shall be provided exclusively in the Member State in which the persons concerned reside, in accordance with its legislation and they have to be provided by and at the expense of the institution of the place of residence. Consequently, the special non-contributory benefits are not exportable and the legislation of the State of residence determines whether a person receives these benefits or not.

In the judgment Kersbergen-Lap and Dams-Schipper[26] the Court of Justice decided that the Wajong benefit was validly qualified as special non-contributory benefit. The Wajong benefit was considered a replacement allowance intended for those who do not satisfy the conditions of insurance for obtaining invalidity benefit. By guaranteeing a minimum income to a socially disadvantaged group (disabled young people), the Wajong benefit is by its nature social assistance justified on economic and social grounds. Moreover, it is granted according to objective criteria defined by law.

351. In the *Hendrix* case,[27] Mr Hendrix lost his job; the reason was that the grant of Wajong meant that the employer was relieved from the obligation of the minimum wage. The benefit supplemented the low wage. After termination of the right to Wajong benefit, the obligation to pay the minimum wage revives. As a result the employer dismissed him. Thus crossing the borders meant that he lost his job. The Court of Justice decided that payment of the Wajong benefit may validly be reserved to persons who reside in the territory of the Member State which provides the benefit. However, the provisions of Regulation 883/2004 enacted to give effect to Article 42 EC, now Article 48 TFEU, must be interpreted in the light of the objective of that Article. This

26. Case C-154/05, [2006] ECR I-6249.
27. Case C-287/05, [2007] ECR I-6909.

objective is to contribute to the establishment of the greatest possible freedom of movement for migrant workers. It follows that the condition of residence attached to receipt of the benefit under the Wajong can be put forward against a person in the situation of Mr Hendrix only if it is objectively justified and proportionate to the objective pursued. It is necessary, the Court continued, that the application of such a condition does not entail an infringement of the rights which a person in the situation of Mr Hendrix derives from freedom of movement for workers which goes beyond what is required to achieve the legitimate objective pursued by the national legislation. It is the responsibility of national courts to interpret, so far as possible, national law in conformity with the requirements of Community law.[28] In the subsequent procedure, the Dutch court decided, taking into account this judgment, that the Wajong benefit had in this case to be exported.[29] This was since terminating benefit in this case can result in the loss of a job, and this is a serious impediment of the right of free movement.

III. The Level of Benefit

352. The level of the disability benefit for the fully disabled amounts to 75% of the minimum wage. An increase to 100% of the minimum wage is possible in cases where the person in question is in a preliminarily permanent situation of invalidity necessitating regular care and nursing (Article 1a:5). Note that minimum wage for adults is payable for persons over 23; lower rates apply for younger ones. .

28. As it had already decided in other cases, e.g., Case C-106/89 *Marleasing* [1990] ECR I-4135.
29. CRvB 7 Feb. 2008, *AB* 2008, 204.

Chapter 4. Pregnancy and Childbirth

353. There are several regulations offering income protection to women who do not work owing to pregnancy or childbirth.

354. Pregnancy and maternity benefits are paid the *Wet Arbeid en Zorg* (Act on Work and Care). The personal scope of the coverage is the same as that of the other employment schemes, such as the ZW, whereas only women are entitled to pregnancy and maternity leave. This means that employees and assimilated persons, such as homeworkers, are covered.

355. Pregnancy and maternity benefit is paid during the duration of the pregnancy and maternity leave, which is sixteen weeks. It is prolonged when the pregnancy leave lasted for more than six weeks, which happens when the delivery takes place at a later date than expected. Pregnancy leave is at least for four weeks and can be for the six weeks prior to the expected date of delivery. When pregnancy leave is less than six weeks, maternity leave is ten weeks plus the number of days pregnancy leave lasted less than six weeks.

356. In the case of adoption, each of the adoptive parents has the right to leave for four weeks, during which time no wage is paid. Instead, they receive benefit during these four consecutive weeks. The purpose of the leave is to enable the parents and child to get accustomed to each other. The adoption leave can be taken from two weeks before the moment the adopted child comes within the care of the adoption parents; this may apply when the parents are abroad. The leave has to be taken within a period of eighteen weeks from the moment of adoption. If a person is entitled to both pregnancy and maternity benefit and to adoption benefit, only the former is paid. In the case of adoption of more than one child at the same time, the leave is given only once.

357. The benefits are administered by the Uwv and are funded by the unemployment fund.

358. Employees and assimilated employees, insofar as they are not excluded from the employees insurance schemes, are entitled to a benefit which is 100% of the wage they earned before the leave.

359. After the WAZ was repealed, self-employed persons were no longer entitled to benefits in case of pregnancy and confinement. This was found unsatisfactory and, as of 4 June 2008, self-employed women are entitled to such benefit under the *Wet arbeid en zorg*. The benefit lasts at least sixteen weeks and is for maximum the statutory minimum wage. A condition for this benefit is that the self-employed person worked at least 1,225 hours in the preceding years. For self-employed persons who worked fewer hours, the benefit depends on the income in the year before the benefit is paid.

360. The scheme is administered by Uwv and paid from the general funds.

Part VI. Industrial Accidents and Occupational Diseases

Chapter 1. Introduction

361. In Part V, concerning Incapacity for work, on disability it was pointed out that the introduction of the WAO Act in 1967 signified the end of distinguishing different categories of insured persons according to whether or not they had become incapacitated as a result of an industrial accident or an occupational disease (*see* paragraphs 237 et seq.).

362. As a result of the equal treatment of insured persons who have become incapacitated, irrespective of the cause of their illness or infirmity, employees affected by an accident or an occupational disease may claim subsequent damages from their employer. This was not possible during the time that employees were insured under the *Ongevallenwet* (Accidents Act).

363. The civil law liability of the employer for the losses incurred by the employee in connection with fulfilling his employment was abolished by the Accidents Act. This was deemed justified by the legislator as the employers were obliged to pay the contributions for the accidents insurance themselves.

364. In current legislation on the insurance against the financial consequences of incapacity to work, the civil law liability of the employer has not been abolished. If the losses incurred are not compensated by payment of wage by the employer on account of Article 7:629 of the BW or by benefits by virtue of the ZW or the WIA, the employee may recover these losses from his employer. If the employer does not or not sufficiently meet his contractual or legal obligations to see to the employee's safety, the employee may demand indemnification from his employer.

365. Chapter 1 will give a summary of the civil law obligations of the employer. In Chapter 2 we shall examine whether this system of civil law obligations suffices to justify the non-existence of a (further-reaching) social insurance scheme.

Chapter 2. Obligations of Employers under Civil Law

366. Article 7:658 BW obliges the employer to furnish and maintain the rooms in which, and the equipment and tools with which, he has the labour performed in such a way, as well as to take such measures and give such instructions as may reasonably be needed, to prevent the employee from being harmed in the course of his work.

The *Arbeidsomstandighedenwet* (Arbo [Working Conditions Act]) and the *Arbeidstijdenwet* (ATW [Working Hours Act]) authorize specified public authorities to lay down further regulations to ensure the safety, to protect the health, and to promote the welfare of the employees in connection with labour. These regulations are a big help in determining the extent of the obligation of the employer to take the relevant measures to prevent accidents, in other words what may reasonably be expected of him.

367. The employee can claim compensation from his employer if he suffers damage in the course of his work (Article 7:658 BW). The employer is liable for this damage unless he proves that he has met his obligation to take sufficient measures to prevent accidents (the 'care obligation'). When the employer uses assistants and charges them with supervising or executing the work to be done, he is as liable for their conduct as he is for his own.

368. If, in the course of his work, the employee falls victim to a risk which the employer could not have foreseen or known, the employer as a rule cannot be held liable for this employee's loss by virtue of the contract of employment. The employer may, however, be liable on account of the fact that he owns things, buildings or animals which the employee has to deal with in the course of his work and by which he is harmed. In those cases, the employee may appeal to the employer's legal liability. It may also be the case that the employer is, after all, deemed liable by virtue of the contract of employment and by the Civil Code if he had failed to take the necessary measures with regard to knowable risks which measures could have prevented the occurrence of the unknowable risk. In recent case law, the employer has been held liable for the development of mesothelioma as a result of asbestos particles in the lungs and the subsequent incapacity to work owing to illness, although the connection between that illness and asbestos was not yet known at the time the employee worked with asbestos. The employer could have known, however, that working with asbestos was hazardous to a person's health and he failed to take the proper measures.

369. The employee cannot hold the employer liable by virtue of the contract of employment in relation to the Civil Code if the loss is largely due to his intent or deliberate recklessness. In case of a lesser degree of culpability on the employee's part, the employer is liable for the total loss, although some more recent case law allows proportional liability in some cases.

Chapter 3. The Absence of a Statutory Insurance Against Industrial Accidents and Occupational Diseases

370. Until 1967 in the Netherlands, in case of employment injury or occupational disease, disabled persons were eligible for benefit on the basis of the *Ongevallenwet* (Accidents Law). In the case of non-work-related incapacity, they had to rely on the *Invaliditeitswet* (Invalidity Law). Benefits on the basis of the first law were considerable higher than those on the basis of the latter. After the Second World War, the feeling grew that benefits on the basis of the *Invaliditeitswet* were in fact too low. Moreover, there were many court actions by persons whose claim to benefit on the basis of the *Ongevallenwet* was refused, as the distinction between work-related disability and non-work-related disability is notoriously difficult to define, as is also known from studies on countries still having this distinction.[30]

Consequently, this system was found to be inconsistent with the new legal basis for social security, as developed during the Second World War. A new law was introduced, the WAO, which came into force in 1967. A main characteristic of the new law was that it no longer distinguished between the different causes of incapacity for work. In other words, since the introduction of the WAO, there is no longer a special benefit for persons who become incapacitated as a result of an accident at work, or a disease arising from work undertaken, or the work environment. The introduction of this law created a unique system. Other countries still make a distinction on the basis of the cause of disability.

Parliament, when adopting the new law, was aware that the ILO conventions make a distinction on the basis of the cause of disability, but Parliament also knew that this distinction is not required, provided that the new law satisfies the requirements of Convention 121.[31]

371. The Netherlands ratified ILO Convention 121, concerning employment injury benefits. As the Netherlands has no special scheme for accidents at work and professional diseases, the WAO, and at present, the WIA have to satisfy the requirements of Convention 121. As a result also the benefits for non-work-related incapacity for work have to satisfy the Convention's requirements.

372. Convention 121 requires, for instance, that there must be no qualifying period for benefit. Consequently, a person who becomes fully disabled on the first day of work is entitled to full benefit.

Convention 121 provides that if a State has a wage-related system, benefit has to be 60% of the last earned wages. If it has a flat-rate scheme, disability benefit has to be 60% of the wage of an ordinary worker.

373. At present there are disputes whether the WIA is fully consistent with Convention 121. One problem is that for the benefit during the first period (the WGA) benefit, the employment past is relevant. This connection of the right to and duration of benefit with the employment record is contrary to Article 9(2) of Convention 121, which provides that eligibility of benefits may not be made subject to the length of

30. See, for instance, N. Harris, *Social Security Law in Context* 492 (Oxford University Press 2000).
31. *Parliamentary Papers II* 1962/63, 7171, Nos 3, 4.

employment, to the duration of insurance, or to the payment of contributions. A second element is that the supplement after the period of WGA benefit depends on having work. Also this is contrary to Article 9(2), as there is a relation between the length of the employment contract and the duration of the supplement.

A third problem is that under the new rules there is a large difference between the partially disabled and the wholly disabled. Article 14 of Convention 121 prescribes that in case of substantial loss of earning capacity likely to be permanent, the benefit shall be a periodical payment representing a suitable proportion of that provided for in paragraph 2 of this Article. The question is, of course, whether the large differences under the new law can still be called 'suitable'.

374. In its 2011 Report on the application of the Conventions, the Committee of Experts concluded that several aspects of the new Dutch Disability Act are not in line with Convention 121.[32] The Committee found the following problems.

According to the WIA, partial disability is recognized and compensated only when 35% or more of earning capacity is lost. The Committee noted that this threshold is set too high to comply with the Convention. A second issue is the level for persons who are fully disabled, i.e., those who have lost at least 80% of their earning capacity. They are entitled to an incapacity benefit of 75% of the monthly wage, which is above the 60% requirement set by the Convention. However, the benefit is reduced by 70% of the income earned by the person from employment or self-employment during the month. The Committee noted that Convention 121 does not authorize any reduction in the benefit in the case that a fully incapacitated person (80%–100% disabled) finds a way to earn additional income from any gainful occupation, leaving him free to combine invalidity benefit with work. Third, persona with a partial disability of between 35% and 80% retains a certain working capacity and is for the remaining part considered to be unemployed. As a consequence s/he is obliged to register as a jobseeker, to make sufficient attempts to obtain suitable work, and to accept an offer of such work – all conditions that normally apply to unemployment benefit recipients. The Committee considered that under such conditions the wage-related WGA benefit falls outside the scope of the Convention because its eligibility requirements are those of the unemployment benefit and not of the employment injury benefit.

A fourth issue is that the entitlement to the WGA benefit is subject to the qualifying period of performing work as an insured person for at least twenty-six weeks during the thirty-nine weeks immediately preceding the loss of entitlement to wages in the case of sickness or to the sickness benefit. Under Article 9(2) of the Convention, eligibility for benefits may not be made subject to the length of employment or the duration of insurance. As the Convention does not permit the benefit to be affected in this way by the length of previous employment, the wage-related WGA benefit can be taken into account for the purpose of the application of the Convention only in its minimum duration of six months.

The wage supplement benefit is further subjected to the income requirement that the insured person partially capable of work must earn, per calendar month, an income from work that is at least equal to 50% of his remaining earning capacity. The requirement to use the residual earning capacity as a condition for entitlement is contrary to the

32. Committee of Experts on the Application of Conventions and Recommendations, *Report III (Part 1A)*, 746 (International Labour Office 2011).

basic philosophy of the Convention, which guarantees benefits at the prescribed level without regard to the residual earning capacity and additional income which can be earned by the workers with incapacity. It appears therefore that only the follow-up WGA benefit can be taken into account for the purpose of the application of the Convention.

The Committee further observed that the disproportionately low level of the follow-up WGA benefit might result, contrary to the objective of Article 14(5) of the Convention, in hardship for many partially disabled persons, obliging them to apply for social provisions or assistance in case they do not find sufficiently paid employment. This is a situation that the Convention was designed to avoid by obliging the ratifying state to institute a scheme that excludes the need for victims of employment injury to have recourse to social assistance.

375. In 2012, the Committee of Experts discussed the required Report of the Netherlands on the WIA.[33] The Committee decided that there were no new elements that would cause it to change its previous conclusions on the WIA. It noted, however, that the Government disagreed with these conclusions and challenged the Committee's understanding of the content of related provisions of the Convention. Since Committee realized that responding in full to the Government's position would require lengthy explanations of the scope and purpose of different provisions of the Convention in the context of the evolution of international social security law a 'light' Direct Mission of the ILO was sent to the Netherlands in July 2012 to discuss the issue with the Ministry of Social Affairs, social partners, benefit administration and academic researchers.

33. Report of the Committee of Experts for the 2012 Conference, Report III (Part 1A), ILC 101/III1A, 876 (International Labour Organization 2012).

Part VII. Unemployment

Chapter 1. Introduction

376. There are several schemes that provide unemployed persons with an income. Some of these regulations are intended to replace the income which has been lost as a result of unemployment. These regulations include the WW. Other regulations provide for a minimum income level. Chapter 2 of this part will discuss the WW. The social minimum schemes will be discussed in Part X.

377. In Chapter 2, before we discuss the WW we will discuss the measures aimed at the reintegration of unemployed jobseekers into work. Chapter 3 deals with the benefit to employees in case the employer is in a situation of insolvency.

Chapter 2. Promotion of Reintegration into Work

§1. Legal Framework

378. Active labour market policy may be described as the whole of measures that are aimed at promoting the employment of (unemployed) jobseekers. Various organizations and bodies are directly involved in the provision of labour and have to cooperate within this framework: in particular the Uwv (Uwv WERKbedrijf and municipalities. The goal, task, organizational structure and financing of this organization are regulated in the Wet Suwi (paragraphs 380 et seq.).

379. The objective of the *Wet Structuur Werk en Inkomen* closely links the payment of benefits and reintegration efforts. This is done through the Uwv WERKbedrijf which social insurance benefit administrations (Uwv and SVB), the municipal agencies for social assistance and the employment offices closely cooperate.

I. Public Employment Services

380. The Uwv WERKbedrijf is charged with public labour exchange and several related tasks on behalf of jobseekers and employers. The law describes the relevant activities which the Uwv WERKbedrijf must perform in each case and states that these activities for employers and employees are free of charge. These activities are as follows:

- establishing and maintaining a decentralized national organization for public labour exchange;
- registering jobseekers;
- registering vacancies;
- drawing jobseekers' attention to suitable vacancies;
- drawing employers' attention to suitable jobseekers;
- collecting and analysing information with regard to developments in the labour market; and
- supplying information and advice on labour market questions, choice of studies and career and retraining and courses and the instruments which are at the disposal of the municipalities and the Uwv to promote the employment of people who are disabled.

381. All persons of Dutch nationality and foreigners who are legally in the Netherlands have the right to register as jobseekers. Furthermore, all employers have the right to register vacancies. Unemployed people are obliged to duly register as jobseekers with the Uwv WERKbedrijf under the unemployment benefit schemes. Employers are not obliged to register their vacancies.

II. Private Employment Services

382. There are many private labour agencies operating in the Netherlands. In order to be allowed to practise their activities, they no longer need a license. Before 2003 such licenses were required.

Private services must not demand quid pro quo from jobseekers for exchange of services rendered. The same applies for public services.

III. Temporary Employment Agencies

383. In the Netherlands, temporary employment agencies play an important role in employing jobseekers. Temporary employment agencies employ people and place them at the disposal of a third party for a remuneration to perform work under this third party's supervision. As of 1998, temporary employment agencies no longer need a license for their activities and a maximum period no longer applies for temporary employment. The obligation to pay the same wage to temporary employees as to employees of the borrowing company who perform similar tasks is, however, maintained. By means of a collective agreement, it is possible to deviate from this rule. In addition, temporary employment agencies must not place employees at the disposal of a company which is involved in a collective labour conflict.

IV. Training while Remaining Entitled to Benefit

A. Unemployment Benefits Act

384. Article 72 WW obliges the Uwv to promote the reintegration into work of WW recipients. This is a general task. The WW mentions a couple of limited facilities for reintegration while in receipt of benefit.

385. Article 76 WW offers unemployed people the opportunity to participate in training which is deemed necessary by the Uwv while remaining entitled to their unemployment benefits.

Beneficiaries participating in the training as meant in Article 76 are exempt from obligations aimed at employment such as the obligation to apply for jobs.

386. The Minister of Social Affairs and Employment has laid down a regulation concerning the nature, substance and duration of the training that can be attended while remaining in receipt of benefit. These regulations require that the training must be a form of systematically acquiring knowledge or skills according to a particular programme by which the acquired knowledge and skills can be tested. The training may not last longer than one year unless the new employer can guarantee a contract of employment for at least six months immediately upon completion of the training at on average the same number of weekly hours of the previous training. Trainees may do productive work only to a limited extent during their training period.

387. Under penalty of total or partial refusal of benefit, a beneficiary can be obliged to participate in a training programme deemed necessary for his employment.

388. A second facility is regulated in Article 76(a) WW. This provision reads that the Uwv can give permission to a beneficiary to do unremunerated work for an employer for a maximum period of six months on a so-called trial job. These have to be activities of which, in the view of the Uwv, there is a real prospect on a job following the trial period of at least the same extent for a period of at least six months.

389. A last facility mentioned in the WW, in Article 77(a), concerns WW recipients who wish to work as self-employed persons. The Uwv can give permission to them to do this work while remaining in receipt of benefit for a maximum period of twenty-six weeks if it is likely that the employee can provide in his income with these activities on a structural basis. A further condition is that the activities must not have started yet when the permission is asked and can be given once only during one benefit period.

B. Public Assistance Act and Other Subsistence Schemes

390. Also, recipients of public assistance schemes (*Participatiewet*, IOAW, IOAZ) can attend training which is deemed necessary for employment. Participation in such a training programme may be made compulsory in order to be or to remain entitled to the benefit concerned. The participant is exempt from a number of obligations aimed at employment such as the obligation to apply for jobs during the training period. The Uwv gives advice to the municipality on whether training is required for employment.

Chapter 3. Unemployment Benefits

391. The WW is a compulsory insurance scheme for the financial consequences of unemployment.

§1. Field of Application

392. Only employees are eligible for unemployment benefit on account of the WW. Under the WW, an employee is defined as the person who has a contract of employment as referred to Article 7:610 of the BW. Various types of labour relations have been put on a par with a contract of employment, subject to certain conditions. Persons are no longer considered to be employees when they have reached the age of 65 (paragraphs 108 et seq.).

393. The concept of employee relevant to the WW largely corresponds with that in the ZW (paragraphs 265 et seq.). A particular feature, however, is that a person remains considered as an employee for the WW even if he is no longer employed, unless he undertakes activities which are not insured by the WW. This is, for instance, the case if the person whose employment has been terminated starts working as a self-employed person. It is also possible to gradually lose the status of employee, i.e., in proportion to the number of hours the concerned person works as a self-employed person. In case one performs voluntary work one does not loses the status of employee anymore for the purpose of the Act, so one can remain entitled to benefit. A regulation of the Minister defines what is meant by voluntary work.

394. If a person loses the status of employee because of doing non-insured activities, he regains the quality of employed person if the activities do not last more than the benefit duration they are entitled to, with a minimum of one-and-a-half years. This means that persons doing self-employed work are still entitled to unemployment benefit if their business fails within this period.

Until 1 January 2015, there were more strict rules, but these have now been amended in order to make taking up work more attractive.

§2. Benefit Rules

I. Conditions

395. Conditions for benefit entitlement are that the person is an employee:

- who is unemployed;
- who is available for work;
- who satisfies the conditions on the work history; and
- there must be no grounds for exclusion.

In the following sections we will discuss the unemployment concept (section A) and its elements (sections B, C and D). Second, we shall pay attention to the conditions on the employment past and the grounds for exclusion (section F). Finally, we shall describe the termination of the entitlement to benefit and the revival of the right to benefit (sections G and H, respectively).

A. Unemployment

396. Article 16 of the WW gives the definition of the term 'unemployment' for this Act. A claimant is unemployed when he has incurred a relevant loss of working hours. In order to be able to speak of unemployment, it is not necessary that the employed person has lost his job completely, so dismissal is not a requirement.

B. Loss of Working Hours

397. With regard to loss of working hours, three questions have to be distinguished: When is there a loss of working hours? How is the number of lost hours calculated? When is the loss relevant to benefit entitlement? These three questions will be answered below.

398. A loss of working hours generally occurs when employment is terminated. A loss of working hours may, however, also occur during employment. This is, for instance, the case if the contract of employment is suspended. Loss of working hours can also occur if the number of working hours is reduced. Unlike under previous versions of the Act, it now provides that a working hour is an hour for which an employee receives income out of work or is entitled to income out of work. Thus it is not sufficient that one does not actually work, but it is relevant whether one loses the right to wage over an hour. In this way persons who do not have to work anymore during a period of notice or during holidays are still considered as working.

Since reduction of working hours can only take place after consent by the employee or a permission of the Uwv WERKbedrijf, a simple loss of working hours is often not sufficient for benefit entitlement, as the Uwv will claim that the employee is still entitled to wage.

399. As a rule, the calculation of the number of lost working hours is as follows:

(1) A calculation has to be made of the average number of working hours of the claimant during the twenty-six calendar weeks immediately preceding the loss of working hours. Only working hours as an employee count. For this purpose, hours in this twenty-six-week period that an employee has received wages without working, and hours during which he has not worked owing to illness or incapacity to work, are considered as working hours; they count towards the average of the past twenty-six weeks.
(2) It is relevant how many hours the person in question still works as an employee in the calendar week in which the loss of working hours occurs.

The difference between the two produces the number of working hours which are lost.

Example. An employee works thirty hours a week until 3 March 2008 and then thirty-five hours a week for four weeks. After these four weeks, he resumes the working pattern of thirty hours a week. The average of this period of twenty-six weeks before 31 March is (22 × 30) and (4 × 35) is 30.7. On 31 March, he works thirty hours again, so his loss is not five hours but 0.7 hours.

There are separate regulations for all kinds of special situations, for example for the calculation of the size of the loss of working hours in case of variable work patterns and for the situation that someone loses part of his work several times in a row.

400. The loss of working hours must be at least five in order to be considered as a relevant loss for benefit entitlement. In the example in paragraph 399, the loss is therefore irrelevant to benefit entitlement.

A loss of less than five working hours is nevertheless a relevant loss if it is at least half of the regular average number of hours per week for this employee. So this rule is relevant only to persons in small jobs.

Example. A person works eight hours a week and loses four hours. This is a relevant loss, and he is entitled to benefit if all other conditions are satisfied as well.

A regulation gives special rules to successive relevant and irrelevant losses of working hours. Otherwise a person who has a forty-hour-a-week job who loses four hours in week A and four hours four weeks later would not be considered unemployed.

401. An employee who is still entitled to wage over lost working hours is, therefore, not unemployed. For the answer to the question whether an employee may claim his full wage without working, Article 7:628 BW is of particular interest. This Article provides that an employee will retain his right to wage if he does not perform the agreed work because of a circumstance which, in all fairness, should be for the account of the employer. In respect of the first six months of the employment, the employer and employee may deviate from this rule by way of a written agreement. After these six months, a deviation from the statutory rules is possible only by way of a collective labour agreement.

402. Article 7:628 BW particularly applies in situations in which the employer terminates the employment relationship while being in conflict with a provision of dismissal law. Important is that an employer who wishes to terminate a contract of employment (without consent of the employee) must have a permit to do so from the Uwv WERKbedrijf or can go to court (which depends on the ground for dismissal). A permit is not required in case of summary dismissal on account of an urgent reason that the employer has immediately communicated to the employee as soon as the reason became known to the employer.

403. An employee may also claim wage and therefore will not be unemployed if no work is done owing to slackness in the business, stagnation in the supply of raw materials, etc. (Article 7:628 BW). Article 7:628 BW also plays a part in situations where an employer suspends or lays off an employee. During the suspension period, there is no unemployment if the employee is entitled to continued payment of wages.

404. Income paid after termination of employment by the employer (severance pay) affects entitlement to benefit if the employer has not observed the appropriate period of notice.

Benefit is not paid during the period of notice which would have applied if the applicable periods would have been applied. The effect of this is that, in most cases, the employee becomes unemployed at a later stage and that entitlement to benefit is postponed. In this case, the employee must in fact use (a part of) the severance payment to bridge the period between the end of employment and the start of the entitlement to unemployment benefit.

C. *Availability for Work*

405. In order to be considered unemployed, an employee must not only have incurred a relevant loss of working hours, but he must also be available for work. An employee is available for work when he is able and willing to accept work on the labour market. So this requirement does not require availability for work as an *employee*.

406. As far as the answer to the question whether someone is available is concerned, it does not matter if the claimant puts restrictions on his availability, even if not medically justified. He may, for instance, be available for work in which he can sit only or for part-time work only. What matters is that the work for which the employee is available exists on the labour market. This broad approach 'opens' the benefit scheme for the person concerned, but his benefit entitlement may be affected by sanction rules, to be discussed below, if his availability is considered insufficient. As a result, benefit may be reduced or even refused completely.

As part of the entitlement conditions, availability must have a certain sense of reality. An employee who is exclusively looking for work which is too cumbersome for him or for which he is lacking the necessary papers is not really available. Similarly, an employee who only wants to work for a specific employer, whereas it is certain that this employer does not want to employ him, is not really available.

407. In case law, availability is characterized as the factual situation the employee is in. The question whether or not an employee is available therefore must be answered on the basis of facts and circumstances of the actual case. The employee's attitude and conduct also play a part in this respect. Whether the employee in question is culpable with regard to his attitude or conduct from the WW viewpoint is, however, not important. If a person cannot help the fact that he is not at all looking for a job, he is still unavailable and, therefore, not unemployed.

D. *Conditions on the Employment Past*

408. During the thirty-six weeks immediately preceding the first day of unemployment, the claimant must have worked as an employee in at least twenty-six weeks. The number of hours or days per week that are worked are irrelevant for this condition. A regulation (*Regeling gelijkstelling niet-gewerkte weken met gewerkte weken* – Decree of assimilation of not-worked weeks with worked weeks) specifies in which situations weeks in which no work was done are assimilated with weeks in which work was done provided that wage was paid in these weeks. A major example is holidays.

409. In addition, the reference period of thirty-six weeks is extended in some circumstances (Article 17(a) WW). This period is extended by a week for each full week that the employee could not do any work, on the grounds specified in the law. Major examples are illness and incapacity. This means that if a person has been ill for ten weeks, the period of thirty-six weeks is extended to forty-six weeks. In the period of forty-six weeks of this example the claimant must have worked in twenty-six weeks. Another example in which the period of thirty-six weeks is extended concerns the situation that a person performed non-insured work and regained the capacity of employee (paragraph 394). Otherwise he would not be entitled to benefit in case he started this work before or on the very day he lost work.

410. In assessing whether an employee has satisfied the condition of having worked in twenty-six weeks, only the employment in which he has become unemployed may be taken into account. Furthermore, weeks that have already been considered for an entitlement to benefit will not be considered for a new claim. In other words, if a person claims benefit for two months, takes up work for two months and then becomes unemployed again, the months before the first claim are irrelevant. He is entitled only to the remaining benefit days of his first entitlement.

411. For some categories of people, such as musicians and other artists, a special rule applies: they have to work sixteen weeks in a period of thirty-nine weeks.

E. Grounds for Exclusion

412. Entitlement to benefit is excluded (Article 19 WW) if, *inter alia*, the employee:

- receives sickness benefit;
- receives WIA benefit;
- receives a WAO benefit or comparable benefit calculated on the basis of a degree of incapacity of 80%–100%;
- is abroad for reasons other than holidays;
- does not legally stay in the Netherlands (according to the Aliens Act);
- has been deprived of his freedom according to the law;
- has reached the first day of the month in which he reaches pension age;
- is on holiday; a regulation gives, however the right to be on holiday for four weeks a year, so this ground applies only if holiday exceeds this period; or
- is unemployed as a result of a strike or lock-out.

F. Termination of Entitlement to Benefit

413. Termination of the right to benefit is regulated in Article 20 of the WW. First of all entitlement ends if the benefit term has lapsed, in other words, if benefit right has been exhausted (*see also* paragraphs 421 et seq.). Entitlement also stops if there are grounds for exclusion (*see* paragraph 412). These grounds for ending the entitlement will be discussed below.

414. As was already discussed above (paragraph 393), a person who is entitled to benefit and starts performing non-insured work loses the capacity of employee to the extent of these activities. As a result, his benefit is reduced proportional to the number of hours of the loss of his quality as employee. For example, for an employee whose entitlement to benefit has been calculated on the basis of a loss of forty working hours, the level of benefit is reduced by 50% if he starts work as a self-employed person during twenty hours a week. Article 77a allows a starting self-employed person, as we have seen, to apply for the alternative method, which takes his income from work into account instead of reducing the number of hours on which his benefit is based.

415. What is to be understood by non-insured work? According to the case law, this is work which has economic value and its performer intends to receive remuneration for this. This may be work as a self-employed person.

416. Performing work as an employed person does – unlike under previous versions of the Act – no longer lead to termination of the right or reduction of the right; instead 70% of the income out of work is deducted from benefit.

G. *Revival of the Right to Benefit*

417. The right to benefit which has been partially or totally terminated before the maximum benefit term has lapsed revives if the circumstance leading to termination of the right has ceased to exist and no new entitlement to benefit has arisen (Article 21 WW). There are a few exceptions to this rule.

418. One of the exceptions is that revival of the right to benefit is in some cases possible only within a specific period after the right has ended.

419. If a person started to work as self-employed and then ends his activities as such, the period is the same as in Article 8 WW, already mentioned in paragraph 393: the maximum period of his benefit duration, with a minimum of one-and-a-half years.

420. A period of six months applies if the right has ended as a result of holidays, detention or staying abroad for reasons other than holidays.

II. The Level and Duration of Benefit

421. During the first two months, benefit is, in case of full unemployment, 75% of the daily wage. After this period, the level is 70%. We will first discuss the duration of benefit (section A) and then a number of special points regarding the benefit's duration and level (section B), the regulation on the determination of the benefit level in case the beneficiary takes up work (section C), and finally, the rules intended to prevent undesirable overlapping of benefit and other income (section D).

422. A person whose benefit is below the applicable subsistence income may be eligible for a supplement on the basis of the TW. When the right to benefit has ended, employees (born before 1965) who have become unemployed after they have reached the age of 50 (together with their spouse if any) may, subject to certain conditions, claim a benefit under the Income Provision for Older and Partially Disabled Unemployed Employees Act (IOAW). One of those conditions is that the (family) income is below the relevant social minimum. Other employees may claim a benefit under the terms of the *Participatiewet* (Public Assistance Act), in which case they have to satisfy a means test on income and capital. These Acts will be discussed in Part X.

423. The duration of benefit is related to the length of the employment past (and age) of the claimant. The minimum duration is three months. This period is longer if, in each of the four calendar years lying in the five calendar years immediately before the first day of unemployment, the claimant received wages over at least 208 hours.

If this condition is satisfied, the duration of benefit is one month for each year that counts for the employment past for the first ten years of work.

424. Thus if the employment past is eight years, the total duration of benefit entitlement is eight months. Years in which over 208 hours wages were received that exceed ten, count for half a month. So after twenty years of work, one is entitled to a benefit of fifteen months. The maximum duration is twenty-four months.

425. This is a less attractive system than before 2015 and currently still transitional rules apply, that provide for longer benefits.

426. For the calculation of the actual working history, days for which a person is entitled to full disability benefit (80%–100%) are assimilated as days for which wage has been received.

427. Also calendar years during which the claimant received child benefits for a child under 5 and did not work count for the employment past, although for 50% only. Thus, this rule applies only if the claimant does not receive wages over at least 208 hours in that particular year. Also assimilation rules apply for persons who, under some conditions, take care of other persons.

428. In case of total unemployment, the benefit is 75% (during first two months) and 70% (later) of the previously earned wage, subject to the statutory ceiling discussed earlier before (EUR 202 a day in 2016).

429. If the right to benefit has ended completely and subsequently revives, the claimant is entitled to the unused days of his entitlement, provided he satisfies the conditions for revival of the right (paragraph 417).

However, if the person received sickness benefit, the first thirteen weeks of the interruption of the right to unemployment benefit do not lead to extension of the benefit period (Article 43 WW).

430. An employee who has not lost all his working hours when he became entitled to benefit or whose entitlement to benefit partly ends on grounds of working or limited availability for work, receives benefit in accordance with his degree of unemployment (number of working hours/non-available hours and total number of working hours at the time he became unemployed).

For instance, if he worked forty hours, lost all these forty hours and was available for twenty hours only, his benefit is 50% of the level he would have received in case of full unemployment and full availability.

431. If a benefit recipient takes up work 70% of the income out of this work is deducted from benefit. Previously there was a more strict rule that reduced the number of working hours that were lost. In case a person took up lower paid work, he could thus be worse off. Moreover if he lost this work, his right did not increase to the previously number of lost working hours and remained at the lower number. This was deemed to be making taking up work unattractive, therefore the current, more simple rules. If the person earns so much that his income is more than 87.5% of the previously earned monthly wage, benefit is terminated completely. However, if the ground for termination does not exist anymore, the benefit right revives, unless the person has acquired a new right.

§3. Obligations

432. The WW contains many obligations for claimants of WW benefit. In view of the way in which violation of these obligations is sanctioned, a distinction may be made between the general obligation to give the benefit administration all relevant information and other obligations.

Violation of the general obligation to provide information is punishable by an administrative fine. If the employee does not comply with the other obligations, no fine but rather an administrative measure is imposed. The Uwv is obliged to impose the measure of fine if the condition of the Act for imposing this sanction is fulfilled. Only in case of urgent reasons may it decide not to impose a measure. A measure is not imposed if a fine has been imposed for the same conduct.

433. In case of violation of some specific obligations to be enforced by measures, the WW explicitly indicates which measure should be imposed. This applies to the obligation for the employee to prevent him from becoming unemployed through his own fault. This is also the case for the employee's obligation to prevent him from becoming or staying unemployed because he neglects to accept suitable work or because he does not obtain or keep suitable work through his own fault. In case of violation of these obligations, the benefit must, as a rule, permanently and completely be refused.

In case of violation of the other obligations to be enforced by measures, the WW does not prescribe what measure should be taken. The law only indicates that the benefit will be temporarily or permanently, totally or partially refused. The Uwv has, however, laid down further rules with regard to the severity of the measures to be imposed.

434. The following paragraphs will first take a brief look at the general obligation of giving information (section I). Second, we shall focus on the employee's obligation not to become unemployed through his own fault (section II). After that we shall deal with the obligations in respect of accepting, obtaining and keeping suitable work (section III). Finally, we shall discuss the other obligations of the employee that are to be enforced by measures (section IV), and we shall pay some attention to the effect of these measures (section V).

I. General Obligation of Informing the Benefit Administration

435. The employee is obliged to notify the Uwv at its request or on his own initiative immediately of all facts and circumstances that, in all fairness, could affect his entitlement to benefit, the assertion of his entitlement to benefit, the level or duration of the benefit or the benefit amount paid to the employee (Article 25 WW).

Violation of this broadly formulated obligation is punishable by an administrative fine of EUR 2,269 at maximum (Article 27(a) WW). The regulation of the fine in

Articles 27(a) and the following of the WW corresponds with that in the ZW (*see also* paragraphs 283 et seq.).

II. Prevention of Culpable Unemployment

436. An employee must prevent that he becomes unemployed through his own fault (Article 24(1)(a) WW). In Article 24(2) WW, the definition of 'culpable unemployment' is given. Two situations (a and b) are distinguished, which shall be referred to further as the a-ground and the b-ground. The a-ground is dealt with in paragraphs 436 et seq. The b-ground is discussed in paragraphs 439 et seq. Subsequently, we shall look at the measures in case of culpable unemployment (paragraph 445).

437. Article 24(2)(a) WW provides that an employee is considered to have become culpably unemployed because of an urgent reason in the sense of Article 7:678 BW and the employee can be blamed for this.

438. This formula was introduced in 2006 to replace the previous text that the employee is culpably unemployed 'if he has behaved in such a way that he could have reasonably understood that this conduct could result in termination of his employment'. The old text was very broad and included numerous types of conduct which could give the employer the cause to terminate the employment, such as insufficient performance, negligence, refusal of work and theft of company property. The conduct of the employee did not have to be very serious – coming too late for work or drinking coffee when this was not allowed could already be sufficient to accept culpable unemployment, provided that an employer could reasonably have decided to dismiss the employee for this behaviour. In order to be punishable the conduct towards his employer must be culpable.

439. The text of Article 24, as discussed in paragraph 438, led to many procedures as employees were forced to make sure that their unemployment was not the result of their behaviour. The broad text led to much legal uncertainty. In order to make the labour market work smoother and to reduce the number of procedures, the text of Article 24(2) was amended, and now the criteria for culpable unemployment are much tighter. In other words, it is made easier for employees to become entitled to unemployment benefit.

440. The reference in Article 24(2) to Article 6:678 BW means that the claimant is considered culpably unemployed only in serious cases of misconduct. This Article gives criteria for summary dismissal and lists grounds for such dismissal, including theft from the employer and violence against the employer and fellow employees. The list is not limitative, but in any case it is clear that the behaviour must be serious.

441. The result of the new formula is that if there is no urgent reason, the employee is not culpably unemployed and there are no problems with benefit. So if there are economic reasons, or if an employee is simply not performing well enough, or whatever situation occurs, there is no culpable unemployment and the employee does not have to fight the dismissal in order to be entitled to benefit. This is a very radical change from the previous approach.

442. Article 24(2)(b) concerns the b-ground. It reads that the employee is culpably unemployed if the employment relationship has ended by or on request of the employee, while continuation would not have resulted in such difficulties for the employee that this continuation could not, in all fairness, have been demanded of the employee.

The b-ground makes clear that in case the employee took the initiative, he is culpably unemployed, or what is called in many foreign systems, voluntarily unemployed. Thus, if the employer took the initiative, the employee is safe. In policy rules of the Uwv, it is even laid down that in case of doubt it is assumed that the employer took the initiative.

In other words, if the employee agrees to resign or cooperates in termination of the employment *at the employer's initiative*, he is safe.

443. Only in case the employee took the initiative for termination of the employment contract is it relevant whether the condition for not accepting culpable unemployment applies: does (continuation) of the employment not result in such difficulties for the employee that this continuation could not, in all fairness, be demanded of him? An employee may have all kinds of motives not to extend or maintain the employment. He may object to (changes in) the kind of work or to (a change in) the circumstances under which the employment is fulfilled. The refusal to continue the employment may also be inspired by personal reasons.

For the question whether an employee has become unemployed through his own fault, it does not matter whether the employee's motives not to continue the employment relationship are understandable or even if they may be considered important. What matters is whether they make up for the disadvantage for the Uwv which results from the end or termination of the employment, i.e., the benefit costs.

444. In general, it will have to be presumed that an employee who resigns is unemployed through his own fault. It is still not considered as culpable unemployment if the employee resigns because – through no fault of his own – his employer has made his life miserable for quite some time and this situation is not expected to improve. This is not too easily accepted.

Examples where it has to be investigated are: an employee who has regularly been the victim of sexual intimidation in the place of work and who, after an incident, resigns; or an employee who resigns because he found out that he is working for a company that serves as a front for a greater whole of companies in which money from the criminal circuit goes round and in which moonlighting takes place on a large scale, may be in a position where continuation of his employment relationship is not required.

445. Urgent reasons of a social nature may lead to resignation, which may not be considered culpable unemployment. These urgent reasons include maintaining family relations. The latter plays a part in situations where a person resigns because he is moving his home with his partner who has accepted a job elsewhere. If it is impossible to travel from the new place of residence to and from work on a daily basis, we cannot speak of culpable unemployment.

446. If an employee is culpably unemployed, the Uwv has to refuse permanently and totally WW benefit (Article 27(1) WW). There is one exception to this main rule. If the employee can only to a very small extent be blamed for non-satisfaction of his obligations, the Uwv will partly refuse the benefit over a period of twenty-six weeks, i.e., by lowering the benefit percentage from 70 to 35. In other words, the employee loses half of his benefit for six months. This exception can be made, for instance, if an employee has resigned without the exception to the sanction being applicable, but his situation is understandable. An example is that of an employee who is required to do work that is detrimental to his health and, instead of refusing the work and offering to do other work, he resigns himself.

III. Accepting, Obtaining and Keeping Suitable Work

447. Not only in case of culpable unemployment does the WW provide what measure has to be taken; the same applies when the employee violates the obligations under Article 24(1)(b2) and (b3) WW. These Articles provide that the claimant must prevent becoming or staying unemployed as a result of neglecting to accept suitable work or of failing to obtain or to keep suitable work through his own fault.

448. The concept of 'suitable work' is described in Article 24(3) WW, which defines suitable work as all work which is suitable given the employee's strength and competence, unless acceptance may not be demanded of him for reasons of a physical, mental or social nature.

If an employee has a weak position on the labour market, he may sooner be expected to accept work which is different from the work he did before or for which he was trained. Strictly personal objections to a job are only rarely accepted.

Further regulations have been drawn up in which the suitable work concept has been made slightly more concrete for certain categories of employees.

449. If an employee does not keep a suitable job through his own fault and he is as a result unemployed, the main rule – as is the case with culpable unemployment – is that the benefit is permanently and totally refused. Only if the employee cannot, to a considerable extent, be held responsible for violating this obligation is a measure of 35% during twenty-six weeks imposed (Article 27(1) WW).

If an employee neglects to accept suitable work or if he fails to obtain suitable work through his own fault and, therefore, remains unemployed, the benefit must permanently be refused over the number of hours for which the entitlement to benefit would have ended if the employee would have accepted or obtained the work in question (Article 27(2) WW).

This measure entails the permanent total refusal of the benefit if the employee has become unemployed while being in full-time employment and he neglects to accept a suitable full-time job. If the employee in question (who is unemployed for forty hours) fails to accept a part-time job of twenty-five hours a week, Uwv will permanently refuse the benefit for 25/40 part.

IV. Other Obligations Enforced by Measures

450. The WW also obliges the claimant to apply actively for work and not to impose requirements on work which make it difficult to get such work (Article 24(1)(b)(1) and (4)).

The employee is, moreover, obliged to cooperate in getting education or training which is considered necessary for his employment or in other activities which are beneficial to his reintegration (Article 26).

The employee must not behave in such a manner which is disadvantageous for the unemployment benefit fund (Article 24(5) WW); this Article makes clear that it is not intended to reduce the room given by the new formula of Article 24(2) as described in paragraph 435. An example of such disadvantageous behaviour is that an employee allows the employer not to observe part or all of the appropriate period of notice. If an employee renounces wage or compensation which can be deducted from the unemployment benefit, this will, in most cases, also be considered as an activity which is disadvantageous for the fund.

451. In addition to the previously mentioned obligations, the WW mentions also obligations for the employee meant to make the administration of benefit easier. These obligations concern actions or omissions by the employee resulting in delaying, hampering or hindering the Uwv's work. Some of administrative obligations must be met within a specific period of time. These concern, among other things, notification of unemployment, submission of a request for benefit, registration as a jobseeker with the Uwv WERKbedrijf, extension of that registration, granting inspection of passport or driver's license and submission of worksheets. A worksheet is a form listing, among other things, questions on work done and income received.

Other obligations are meant to make the administrative process easier. For example, if the Uwv feels this is necessary, the employee is obliged to report in on a daily basis, to be at home at specific times, to see to it that, in his absence, housemates are informed of his whereabouts or to subject him to other verification measures related to availability and presence. The employee must also comply with the Uwv's request to appear at a designated place and time and to grant inspection of books, papers and other documents.

452. If the employee does not (duly) comply with the obligations in paragraphs 449 and 450, the Uwv has to impose measures on the claimant, which means that it has to totally or partially, permanently or temporarily refuse the unemployment benefit. The measure has to be in line with the seriousness of the conduct and the degree of culpability of the claimant. As remarked before (paragraph 527), the institution may only decide not to impose a measure in case of urgent reasons.

453. Regulations have been laid down which define in principle which measure has to be imposed as a response to which type of behaviour. These regulations divide the obligations into five categories, with a corresponding standard measure. The seriousness of the facts determines the classification of a certain obligation into a category. Violation of an obligation from the first category is the least serious. Violation of an obligation from the fifth category is the most serious. This is expressed by the level of the standard measures belonging to the categories in question. In case of recidivism, the standard sanction is raised. A lower sanction is imposed if the degree of culpability occasions this. For example, the obligation to make a claim for benefit in time is an obligation which has been included in the fourth category. In case this obligation is not (duly) complied with, the Uwv must reduce the benefit percentage by 20% (from 70% to 50%) during a sixteen-week period. If there is a diminished culpability on the part of the offender, the measure amounts to 10% during sixteen weeks. In case of recidivism within two years, the measure will consist of a reduction of the benefit percentage by 30% during sixteen weeks. If the person in question does not observe the obligation to apply for a third time within twelve months, the benefit will be completely refused for the remainder of the period.

V. The Effect of a Measure after Revival of the Right to Benefit

454. A measure only has effect as long as the person in question is entitled to benefit. The measure can no longer harm the person in question if he is no longer entitled to benefit, for instance because he found a new job. If this new job is lost and, as a result, his entitlement to benefit revives, the Uwv is, however, obliged to continue to refuse the benefit. This refusal, however, may not be continued if the person in question meanwhile has worked as an employee during twenty-six weeks, as in this case he has become entitled to a new right to benefit, since he has now again satisfied the conditions on the employment past. A person therefore can get around a measure that has been imposed by being employed for six months (Article 28 WW).

§4. Benefit in Case of Unworkable Weather Conditions

455. Article 18 of the WW provides that a person is entitled to benefit when he is unemployed on account of frost, snow, high water or other exceptional natural circumstances for the duration of these circumstances. The benefit amounts to 70% of the daily wage of the employee concerned.

456. In this case, all elements of the unemployment concept of the WW have to be fulfilled (paragraph 396), such as that he must have lost at least five working hours per week. The Uwv, however, is authorized to lay down regulations with regard to one or more specific groups of employees on the basis of which an employee who has lost less than five working hours per calendar week is also considered unemployed when a decision has to be made concerning a benefit for unworkable weather.

§5. Voluntary Insurance

457. The WW provides for the opportunity for a voluntary insurance for some categories (Articles 53 and the following). The group of persons who, at their request, have to be included in the voluntary insurance of the WW is relatively small in comparison with that of the ZW and the WAO (paragraphs 154 et seq.). A person who is included in the voluntary insurance of benefit in case of unemployment is considered an employee for the duration of that insurance. A person who requests admission to the voluntary insurance will – within certain limits – determine the level of the daily wage at the start of the insurance. The contribution for the voluntary insurance is levied over the indicated daily wage, and the benefit is calculated on the basis of that daily wage. If necessary, the stipulations concerning the compulsory insurance of benefit in case of unemployment apply accordingly to the voluntary insurance, insofar as these have not been deviated from.

Chapter 4. Insolvency of the Employer

458. The risk of inability of the employer to pay is entirely different from the risk of unemployment. For reasons of efficiency, the legislator has opted for including the insolvency rules in the WW. These rules implement Council Directive 80/987/EEC of 20 October 1980 on the approximation of the laws of the Member States relating to the protection of employees in the event of the insolvency of their employer.

§1. Scope

459. Only employees are entitled to an insolvency benefit. The meaning of 'employed person' is the same as for compulsory unemployment benefit (paragraph 392) with one exception: the 65-year age limit does not apply for insolvency. The Act uses the term 'benefit', but it is no unemployment benefit but a compensation of the not paid wages. If the person later has to apply for unemployment benefit, the already paid benefits are not deducted from unemployment benefits.

§2. Conditions

460. Articles 61 and 62 of the WW state the conditions for the entitlement to benefit in case of insolvency. The employer has to be declared bankrupt to be granted suspension of payment or must otherwise be in a position in which he has permanently stopped all payments. A second condition for benefit is that the employee is entitled to claim wage, holiday pay or holiday allowance from his employer or that he can incur a loss because the employer has not paid sums he owed to a third party on account of the employment relationship (like pension contributions).

A third requirement is that the employment relationship may not have ended before the employer came into the situation that he stopped making payments. There are, however, several exceptions to this rule. This requirement does not apply, for instance, if there is an obvious connection between the circumstances leading to the termination of the employment and the circumstances inducing the employer's insolvency. The requirement also does not apply if the employee cannot assert his claims to wage arrears or other claims solely because of his employer's inability to pay.

461. The law assumes that there is always a permanent situation in which the employer has become insolvent if a court has declared bankruptcy or has granted the employer suspension of payment. Bankruptcy concerns the debtor's entire capital and is aimed at selling all the debtor's goods and distributing the proceeds among the creditors. Employees have a privileged position in this distribution with regard to wage demands for the current and previous years. A trustee is appointed at the bankruptcy decree. The trustee is charged with managing and liquidating the bankrupt's appropriable property.

462. In case of suspension of payment, the court appoints a receiver who, together with the debtor, will administer his enterprise. During the period of suspension of payment, no claims may be laid on the debtor. This does not apply, however, to claims that take precedence. The wage of the debtor's employees therefore will have to be paid as usual. Although suspension of payment is intended to prevent bankruptcy, in reality it can hardly be avoided.

463. It is fairly easy to ascertain whether we are dealing with bankruptcy or suspension of payment, as it is based on a court decision. It is much more difficult to determine whether the employer is otherwise in a position where he has permanently stopped payments. Jurisdiction requires this situation to be caused by inability to pay. There is no room for providing a benefit if the reason that the employer is not paying his employees' wages is not inability but simply unwillingness to do so. The same applies when the employer has not paid wage because he has chosen to utilize the available funds for other purposes.

464. According to the case law, the take-insolvency rules of Articles 61 et seq. of the WW do not apply in situations in which employment has ended in another way than by termination of the contract and in which the employer could not have responded to his inability to pay by a lawful resignation, for instance because the discharge ban during illness (Article 7:670, paragraph 3, BW) made this impossible.

§3. Benefit in Case of Insolvency

465. Articles 61 and 62 of the WW provide the conditions for benefit in case of insolvency. Article 64 WW regulates the contents of the benefit. The benefit first of all includes all wage arrears over the thirteen weeks immediately preceding the day the employment was terminated. In addition, the Uwv has to pay the wage arrears over the period of notice applicable to the employee. In this respect, the period of notice of Article 40 of the Bankruptcy Act is the maximum, both in and outside of bankruptcy. This rule indicates that, in any case, the trustee may dismiss the employees with a six-week notice period.

In the third place, the benefit includes the sum in holiday pay and holiday allowance payable by the employer over the last year and the money he owed a third party over the last year in relation to the employment (such as pension contributions).

466. Article 64 of the WW shows that, when calculating the periods over which wage arrears are paid, the day of termination of the employment relationship is the focal point. The day of termination is the day on which lawful resignation, under civil law, took place. If the employer has terminated the employment without the necessary dismissal permit of Article 6 of the BBA (*see also* paragraph 402), but if he obtains such permit at a later stage, the day on which the previous (invalid) termination was given is deemed to have become effective by conversion (Article 3:42 BW). In other words, this is considered as the day of termination. This is the day that the employee has been able to know that there is a permit for dismissal. For that matter, it should be remarked that in case of bankruptcy of the employer, the trustee who wishes to terminate the employment does not need a permit for dismissal (Article 6(2) BBA).

467. If the employment has not been terminated, or if it has been terminated at a later point in time than the moment which would, in all fairness, be appropriate, the Uwv is authorized under Article 64 of the WW to designate a day on which the employment should reasonably have been terminated.

§4. Obligations

468. The Uwv must totally or partially, temporarily or permanently refuse to pay the benefit in case of inability to pay if the employee of the employer who is incapable to pay is late in informing Uwv that timely payment of the wage and related sums (such as due compensations) by the employer did not take place. Payment of the benefit should also be refused if, before the employment relationship started or before labour conditions were changed, the employee could, in all fairness, have known that, as a result of the employer's insolvency, no wage or only part of it would be paid (Article 63 WW). In addition to violation of these obligations specifically concentrating on the benefit in case of inability to pay, the provision that the employee must not conduct an act of prejudice towards the unemployment benefits fund (paragraph 449) may also be a reason for refusal of the benefit.

A fine is imposed if the person in question has not (properly) observed his general obligation of informing Uwv (paragraph 434). This is a result of Article 68 of the WW, in which many articles on the compulsory unemployment benefit scheme are declared accordingly applicable to the insolvency benefit.

§5. Recovery Insolvency Benefits from the Employer

469. Article 66 of the WW provides that, insofar as the Uwv settles a claim of a creditor (e.g., the employee) in accordance with Articles 61 et seq. of that Act, it will then take over all rights the creditor has with regard to that claim.

Part VIII. Pensions

Chapter 1. Introduction

470. The AOW provides for an old-age pension for everyone who has been insured in the Netherlands. The pension level is related to the minimum wage and further depends on the period of insurance in the Netherlands. In addition, the AOW provides a supplementary benefit on top of the old-age pension if the person entitled to pension has a partner who has not yet reached the age of 65 and who has no income (or a very small one) of his/her own (although this supplement is being phased out). The AOW is a national insurance scheme.

471. Another national insurance scheme is the Anw. This Act provides a benefit to survivors of a person who resided in the Netherlands at the time of his decease. Survivors with an unmarried child may also claim a semi-orphan benefit. The Anw also has a benefit for full orphans. The benefits are related to the minimum wage.

472. The AOW and Anw provide for a minimum income only. Occupational insurance schemes, which provide for wage-related pensions, are not compulsory. Nevertheless, there are numerous pension schemes within the business and professional sectors. The legislator has left the development of these schemes to the business and professional groups themselves. There are, however, statutory regulations stipulating how these agreements have to be observed and what obligations apply for proper management and sufficient supervision. A regulation which has been developed for a specific branch of industrial or professional life may, at the request of certain parties, be declared generally binding for the branch concerned with the Minister of Social Affairs and Employment. We will not describe these provisions here.

Chapter 2. General Old-Age Pension Act

473. The AOW was adopted in 1956. The Act may be considered as the successor of the 1913 *Invaliditeitswet* (Invalidity Act), which provided for an old-age pension at the age of 65 in addition to an invalidity pension and a pension for survivors. The AOW constitutes, however, an important extension of the group of insured persons, since it was not limited to employees anymore.

The AOW is a compulsory insurance for all residents of the Netherlands. It provides a pension, the level of which is related to the statutory minimum wage. The benefits are paid by the SVB. The Tax Office collects the contributions for funding this scheme.

474. In 1985, the AOW was reformed radically. These changes were necessary in connection with EEC Directive 79/7 regarding the equal treatment of men and women in the field of social security. Before, married women were, in principle, not entitled to benefit under the AOW. Married men received a higher pension than single ones. This was contrary to the directive. The law has been changed in such a way that currently everyone who has been insured will receive his own entitlement to pension. In 2012, the Act was reformed again by raising pension age, *see* paragraph 476.

§1. Scope

475. The AOW is a national insurance scheme which is compulsory for all residents of the Netherlands. Also insured are those persons who are not residents but who are subject to wage tax (Article 6) in connection with the work done as employees in the Netherlands. The group of persons covered by the national insurance scheme has already been discussed in paragraphs 83 et seq.

Payment of old-age pension is suspended if it has been granted to foreigners who do not stay legally in the Netherlands. Resumption of payment of old-age pension will occur at the request of the interested party if it has been proven that he is de facto living or staying outside of the Netherlands.

§2. Old-Age Pension

I. Conditions

476. In order to qualify for old-age pension, a person must have reached pension age and must have been insured at least one year (Article 7). Since 1957 pension age had been 65, but as from 2013 this has changed. During the past decade there were extensive discussions on the pension age, since life expectancy has risen considerably since 1957 and the resulting greying of the population meant that relatively fewer persons paid for the costs of the scheme. Therefore it was argued that the scheme as it was could not be maintained. By adopting an amending Act of 2012 the rules on the pension age were changed. Pension age will be gradually increased. As from 2013 it has increased according to the below table.

Year	*Pension Age*	*Starting Age for Insurance*
Before 1 January 2013	65	15
2013	65 + 1 month	15 + 1 month
2014	65 + 2 months	15 + 2 months
2015	65 + 3 months	15 + 3 months
2016	65 + 6 months	15 + 6 months
2017	65 + 9 months	15 + 9 months
2018	66	16
2019	66 + 4 months	16 + 4 months
2020	66 + 8 months	66 + 8 months
2021	67	17

For the years after 2021, pension age will continue to be increasing, depending on the expected life expectancy, as calculated by the Office for Statistics (CBS). The Act (Article 7a) already has a formula for connecting these data to pension age.

Whether a person has reached pension age will be verified by the SVB. In most cases, this will be done by means of data from the civil register. It may be difficult to obtain the correct information if a claimant was born in a country where there was no register at the time or if the register does not accurately state the date of birth. In that case, other data have to be used to clarify matters, such as a passport, a marriage certificate or a church register.

477. In order to be able to claim old-age pension, the person in question does not have to be insured at the time he reaches pension age. It is sufficient that he was insured for at least one year between the starting age (*see* table *supra* and pension age. Consequently, there is no need for an uninterrupted insurance period of fifty years. The insurance may start at a later date; it may have been interrupted by a temporary stay abroad; or it may have been terminated before pension age because the person in question has gone abroad.

II. The Level of the Pension

478. The level of the old-age pension is related to the minimum wage and further depends on the household of the person who is entitled to pension (Article 9). The pension ends when the beneficiary dies. The old-age pension is built up over the course of time: the longer the insurance has lasted, the higher the pension amount the person in question will receive when he has reached pension age (with a maximum of 50 years). The pension is granted irrespective of the income of the entitled person or that of his spouse.

There is no need to stop working in order to be entitled to benefit, although most persons indeed stop working, as their contract of employment ends when they reach pension age. This rule has been disputed in recent years, but so far it has been maintained. Instead an act has introduced provisions that derogate from some labour law rules for persons resuming work after pension age. This makes it more attractive for employers to take on these workers. Examples are that the rules on renewal of fixed-term contracts do not apply and the rule on continued sick pay does not apply for more than six weeks.

In the following paragraphs, we shall first look at the maximum benefit amounts payable under the AOW. After that, we shall discuss the relation between level of pension and insured periods.

A. Maximum Amounts

479. Married persons who are entitled to pension may each claim an old-age pension of 50% of the statutory minimum wage. The level of the old-age pension of single persons who are entitled to pension is 70% of the minimum wage. If a single person supports a child younger than 18, old-age pension amounting to 90% of the minimum wage is paid.

480. A married man or woman who is permanently separated from his/her spouse (for instance, if one of them is in a nursing home) is considered to be single as far as the AOW is concerned.

Two persons who are officially registered as partners are considered married. The same applies to single persons of the same or different sex who conduct a permanent joint household; they are considered married. Consequently, two brothers or sisters or a grandparent and a grandchild having a joint household are considered as married under the Act. The only exception concerns a household of parent and child (related to the first degree). The joint household concept has the same meaning as that under the *Participatiewet* (paragraphs 592 et seq.). If married persons are no longer living together they are not treated anymore as married; this is relevant when one person of a married couple has to move to a nursing home.

481. A person who is entitled to AOW pension and who is living abroad or staying there for more than three months receives a pension amounting to 50% of the minimum wage (Article 9(a)); this means that also single persons receive the (individual) married person's rate.

The rule does not apply for a person who lives in a country with which the Netherlands made an agreement on the administration of benefits, including all European Economic Area (EEA) and EU Member States.

If a person lives outside the Netherlands but stays in the Netherlands for more than three months, he receives the single's pension rate during this period.

B. Reductions

482. There are two cases in which the old-age pension is reduced. A reduction of 2% is applied for each year that the person entitled to pension has not been insured after the starting age and before pension age. A reduction is also applied for each year after the starting age that the entitled person has culpably neglected to pay contributions.

The Tax Office, which collects the AOW contributions, informs the SVB of contributions which in its opinion cannot be recovered. The SVB will then establish whether there is culpable negligence and keep record of this. A person who is temporarily not insured because of residing or working abroad can buy a voluntary insurance. If the AOW pension plus other income (e.g., supplementary pensions) is below subsistence level, this can be supplemented on the basis of the *Participatiewet*. This is also true for persons coming from a country where there was no or a very low pension system, e.g., third country nationals. This benefit is for this group also paid by the SVB. Although the amounts of these benefits are the same there is still a difference since the *Participatiewet* takes other income into account as well as capital.

483. As the AOW came into force in 1957, it contains a transitional provision on behalf of those persons who, by that time, had already reached the age of 15 and thus could never satisfy fifty years of insurance. The period between the day on which one turned 15 and the date the Act became effective (1 January 1957) is considered as the fictitious insurance term for all persons who have lived in the Netherlands for six years after having completed their 59th year. By general legislative measure, it is provided under what conditions persons who do not satisfy these conditions are treated as persons who satisfy the conditions. Also Regulation 883/2004 is relevant to this assimilation.

§3. The Supplement Payable on Basis of the AOW

484. Subject to certain conditions, a person entitled to a pension who is married to someone who has not yet reached pension age may claim a supplement on top of his old-age pension. The purpose of this supplement is that two spouses, of which the young one does not have an income or only a low one, have a joint income which is at least equal to the statutory minimum wage. As soon as the younger partner has reached pension age the supplement is no longer paid and both spouses can each claim a pension amounting to 50% of the minimum wage.

I. Conditions

485. The first condition for the entitlement to a supplement is that the person entitled to an AOW pension is married – in the meaning of this Act – to someone who has not yet reached pension age. As previously indicated in paragraph 479, a married man or woman who is permanently separated from his spouse is considered single as far as enforcement of the AOW is concerned. Unmarried persons who are officially registered as partners or who have a joint household are considered married for this Act.

486. A second condition for the entitlement to a supplement is that the spouse has no income of his/her own or a monthly income which is less than 50% of the statutory minimum wage per month. When answering the question whether the spouse has an income of his/her own, only wages earned within business and professional life may be taken into account and not income from capital.

Of this income, an amount equalling 15% of the minimum wage is left outside of consideration. Of the remainder, a third part is left outside of consideration (Article 11).

487. Entitlement to a supplement is excluded during the period that the person entitled to AOW is living outside the Netherlands or is staying there for more than three months (Article 8a). This rule does not apply to persons entitled to pension who are living outside the Netherlands, but who are staying in the Netherlands for more than three months or who are living in a country with which the Netherlands made a special agreement (including all EEA Member States).

488. The AOW provides that only those persons who reach pension age before 1 January 2015 are, in principle, entitled to a supplement. In other words, those who were born after 1950 will be excluded from the entitlement to a supplement when they reach the age of 65 in 2015 or later.

II. The Amount of the Supplement

489. The maximum amount of the supplement is 50% of the statutory minimum wage. The part of the spouse's income which must be taken into account will be deducted from the supplement (Article 10). In addition, there will be a 2% reduction of the supplement for each year that the partner has not been insured or has been culpably negligent in paying contribution after having reached the starting age of insurance but before the day that the person entitled to pension has reached pension age (Article 13). On the basis of transitional provisions (Article 55) and subject to certain conditions, non-insured years between the date on which the spouse has reached the age of 15 and the date the AOW became effective (1 January 1957) are considered as years in which the spouse *was* insured under the law.

§4. Obligations

490. The AOW imposes obligations on the beneficiary, his partner, as well as his legal representative. The first obligation of importance is the general obligation of informing the SVB of all relevant information. Violation of this obligation is punishable by an administrative fine. The other obligations to be observed by the beneficiary, his partner and his legal representative are stated in the verification regulations of the SVB. These verification regulations have been developed on the basis of Article 15 The verification regulations are not enforced by an administrative fine but by an administrative measure. This measure consists of the total or partial, temporary or permanent refusal of the old-age pension.

I. The General Obligation to Inform the Benefit Administration

491. The beneficiary, his partner, as well as his legal representative are obliged to notify the SVB at its request or forthwith of their own accord of all facts and circumstances which could, in all fairness, obviously affect the entitlement to benefit, the level of the benefit or the benefit amount paid (Article 49).

492. Violation of the general obligation of notification is punishable by a fine. The regulation of the fine in Articles 17(c) and the following show, among other things, that the SVB is obliged to impose a fine. Only in case of urgent reasons may the SVB decide not to impose a fine. The maximum fine amount is the same as the benefit that was unduly paid.

II. Obligations Enforced by Measures

493. The verification regulations contain obligations aimed at streamlining the administrative process within the SVB. These obligations concern actions or negligence of the beneficiary, his partner or legal representative which cause the SVB's activities to be delayed, hampered or hindered. The verification regulations state, among other things, that changes in address and social-fiscal number must be communicated within four weeks (Article 3). At the SVB's request, information must be supplied in due time with regard to the income of the partner of the person entitled to pension over periods that this person has not yet reached pension age. Also pieces of evidence on the partner's income and concerning the joint household have to be submitted at the SVB's request within a fixed period of time (Article 4). The verification regulations further contain rules on granting inspection of books, documents and other information carriers, on submission of current proof of identification and of a document proving that the claimant and their partners who are staying abroad are still alive (Article 5). And, finally, the verification regulations stipulate that beneficiaries and their partners have to obey a summons to appear and to submit any data that may be required (Article 6) and that verification must be made possible (Article 7).

494. In accordance with Article 17b, the SVB must impose a measure if the beneficiary or the partner has not (properly) complied with the SVB's verification regulations.

The measure consists of a sanction in the form of total or partial, temporary or permanent refusal of old-age pension. Only in case of urgent reasons may the SVB decide not to impose a measure. A measure is not imposed if the same conduct is punishable by a fine. Further regulations have been laid down with regard to the severity of the measure to be imposed.

§5. Voluntary Insurance

495. In addition to a compulsory insurance, the AOW also has a voluntary one. The voluntary insurance is of great importance as it may prevent reductions on the old-age pension and the supplementary benefit on account of non-insured years. The voluntary insurance was discussed earlier in paragraphs 101 et seq.

Chapter 3. General Survivors' Insurance

496. Since the beginning of the twentieth century, the care for employees' survivors has been the subject of statutory regulations. The 1901 *Ongevallenwet* (Accidents Act) and the 1913 *Invaliditeitswet* (Invalidity Act) – Acts which demonstrated a strong affinity to the legislation that Bismarck had established in Germany – included pension rights for the insured employee's wife and children in case of his death. The level of the pension in the Accidents Act depended on the wage earned by the employee and in the Invalidity Act mainly on the duration of the insurance and the level of the contributions paid. The nominal value of the pension amounts which had thus been calculated stayed the same, but the actual value became less and less as a result of rises in prices and wages. Consequently, it became more and more difficult for widows and orphans to support themselves with the pension money.

497. After the Second World War, it was decided to improve the position of the widows and orphans as soon as possible. A national insurance scheme was introduced on the recommendation of the committee which had advised the Dutch government in London during the Second World War (paragraph 16). The AWW came into force in 1959. The Accidents Act and the Invalidity Act were abolished in 1967 and replaced with the WAO.

498. The AWW granted a right to benefit to women who were widowed as a consequence of the fact that their insured husbands had died. A widow should, moreover, have reached the age of 40, be incapacitated to work or have an unmarried child. The law provided a widow's pension, the level of which depended on the statutory minimum wage. The pension was granted irrespective of the fact whether the widow had an income of her own. Underaged children of an insured person who had been orphaned because of his death were entitled to orphan's allowance.

499. In 1996, the AWW was replaced by the Anw. This was considered necessary because the circumstances of the society have changed radically: when women get married, they no longer automatically give up their jobs in order to exclusively do the housekeeping. Husband and wife often have their own income and are jointly responsible for financing the household. A second reason was that joint households currently consist more and more often of persons who are not married.

From an economic point of view, the situation of unmarried people living together is not different from that of married people living together. A third reason for replacing the AWW was that, if the husband died, his wife was entitled to pension, but if the wife died, her husband was not. This unequal treatment was considered to be in conflict with the prohibition on discrimination required by Article 26 of the International Treaty on Civil and Political Rights by the Central Appeals Court. This judgment resulted in the situation that, in case one of the spouses died, husband or wife, the other spouse was entitled to pension, irrespective of the question whether he needed such a pension or not.[34] In view of the financial consequences of equal treatment of men and women for the fund from which benefits were financed, the legislator deemed it necessary to develop an entirely new Act: the Anw.

34. CRvB 7 Dec. 1988, RSV 1989/67.

500. The new Act, the Anw, which became effective in 1996, provides benefits to the survivors of a person who was insured at the time of his death. There are three kinds of benefits for survivors: the survivors' benefit, the semi-orphan's benefit and the orphan's benefit. The SVB is charged with preparing, taking and implementing decisions with regard to providing the above-mentioned benefits. The Tax Office levies and collects the contributions for funding this benefit.

§1. Scope

501. The Anw is a national insurance scheme. All residents of the Netherlands are compulsorily insured. In addition, those people are insured who are not residents of the Netherlands, but who are subject to tax on wage in respect of work done as an employed person in the Netherlands (Article 13). The group of persons insured was already dealt with in paragraphs 83 and the following. A special feature of the Anw is that the insurance of a person who starts living abroad and who is not covered by a similar foreign regulation is not terminated until six weeks after the time his residency has ended. This Act, therefore, has an after-effect.

§2. Survivors' Benefit

I. Conditions

A. Who Is Considered a Survivor?

502. Only survivors are entitled to a survivors' benefit. A survivor is defined as the spouse of the person who is insured under the Anw on the day that he dies. The 'spouse' concept first of all indicates the spouse in the civil law sense. It is irrespective of sex, i.e., the survivor may be male or female, so in case of death of a male insured person, his widow may claim survivors' benefit and, in case of death of a female insured person, her widower may do the same, provided that also the other conditions are satisfied.

503. As discussed above, for determining who is a spouse, first of all married persons are taken into account. For the Anw, several other persons are regarded as spouses. First of all, this applies to the person who is officially registered as a partner of the insured person. Consequently, if two persons are engaged in an officially registered partnership, and one of them dies, the other one must be considered a survivor. Second, this applies to an unmarried person who has a joint household with another person, unless it concerns a relative in the first degree. In other words, two people of the same or different sex who are not married to each other and who have a joint household are considered married under the Anw. When one of the two unmarried partners who are living together dies, the surviving partner is, therefore, in principle entitled to survivors' benefit. However, a parent and his (underage) child are not considered to be married even though they have a joint household. The same applies to the survivor who has a joint household with the deceased persons' or his own children, stepchildren or foster children over 18.

504. The definition of common household under the Anw is similar to that of the *Participatiewet* (paragraphs 592 et seq.).

505. Unlike many other social security Acts, the Anw does not consider permanently separated spouses equal to unmarried people. If a couple is permanently separated and one of them dies, the survivor therefore may be entitled to survivors' benefit. There is, however, one exception to this rule. If one of the permanently separated spouses has a joint household with a third party, this person cannot claim survivors' benefit as a result of the death of the other spouse.

506. Subject to certain conditions, the man or woman who was married to the deceased insured person and who divorced, but who has not remarried, is considered the survivor. This person is sometimes called pseudo-survivor. One of the conditions to be entitled to benefit in this capacity is that the deceased insured person had to pay alimony to his former spouse immediately preceding his death. A second condition is that the person in question would have been entitled to survivors' benefit if the former spouse had died on the day the marriage was dissolved (Article 4 Anw).

B. Categories of Survivors

507. Article 14 Anw lists the conditions for the entitlement to survivors' benefit. There are three categories of survivors who are entitled to survivors' benefit.

508. The first category consists of survivors who have an unmarried child under the age of 18 who does not belong to another person's household. Article 5 of the Act provides that this must be a natural child, a stepchild or a foster child who was born before or on the day the insured person died. If a woman is expecting a child when her husband dies, that child is considered to be born on the day the insured person died. A child may only be considered a foster child if the survivor took care of it as a parent at the time the spouse died.

509. Survivors who are incapacitated to work may also claim survivors' benefit. They must (have) be(en) incapacitated on and since the day of the insured person's death. Entitlement to survivors' benefit also exists if the survivor is incapacitated on and since the last day of the month in which he no longer meets the requirement of having an unmarried underage child who does not belong to another person's household. It is, however, required that the survivor is at least 45% incapacitated to work (Article 11) and that, on the day in question, this incapacity has lasted at least three months or that it is likely to last another three months. The incapacity to work concept in the survivors' insurance corresponds to that of the WIA (paragraphs 295 et seq.).

510. The third and last category of people entitled to survivors' benefit is made up of survivors who were born prior to 1 January 1950. The rationale for this rule is that persons belonging to this category often have a bad position on the labour market.

C. Grounds for Exclusion

511. The Act lists a number of situations in which a survivor is not entitled to survivors' benefit (Article 15 Anw). Not entitled is the survivor whose spouse has died within a year after he married that spouse and the death was to be expected in view of the spouse's health at the time of the wedding. If the insured person died because of an unexpected reason, such as a car accident, this does not impede entitlement.

Another ground for exclusion mentioned in the Anw exists if the survivor is the perpetrator of, or the accomplice in the murder of the spouse. And, finally, entitlement to survivors' benefit is also excluded if the spouse's death occurs in or after the month in which the survivor reaches the age of 65. There are, however, several exceptions to some of the above-mentioned grounds for exclusion.

A survivor who has a joint household with another person is excluded from entitlement to survivors' benefit. However, the survivor may claim survivors' benefit if the joint household comes to an end within six months after the spouse has died. The period of six months may be prolonged by the SVB in cases of hardship.

There are several exceptions to the rule. The survivor may not claim survivors' benefit if he has a joint household with another person. Entitlement to survivors' benefit is not excluded if the survivor is in need of care and has started the joint household with another person with a view to be taken care of by that person. Entitlement to survivors' benefit is also not excluded if the survivor or the deceased insured person had started a joint household with a person who is in need of care with a view to take care of that person. Under the terms of the Anw, a person is considered to be in need of care if, due to illness or physical, psychological or mental infirmities, he is not capable to do his own household on a permanent basis, because he is in need of intensive care from other persons.

512. Entitlement to survivors' benefit is excluded for the period that the survivor is living outside the Netherlands or staying there for more than three months. The exclusion ground does not apply to survivors who are living abroad and who are staying in the Netherlands for more than three months. Nor does it apply in case the country concerned has a treaty with the Netherlands on the maintenance of benefit rules (which applies to all EEA Member States).

D. Ending and Revival of the Right to Benefit

513. Article 16 of the Anw provides when the entitlement to survivors' benefit ends. In the first place, the entitlement ends if the survivor no longer has an unmarried child or is no longer at least 45% incapacitated to work, unless the survivor was born before 1 January 1950.

In the second place, the entitlement ends if the survivor gets married, enters in an officially registered partnership or starts a joint household with another person, except in case the joint household was started with a view to taking care of a person who is in need of care (*see* paragraph 62). Entitlement to survivors' benefit which came to an end because the survivor started a joint household revives if the joint household comes to an end within six months after the termination of the survivors' benefit. The SVB may prolong the six months' period in cases of hardship.

514. Furthermore, the entitlement ends if the survivor reaches pension age. Entitlement to survivors' benefit is also terminated if the survivor goes abroad and it revives as soon as he takes up residence in the Netherlands. If he lives in a country with which the Netherlands has made an agreement, benefit is not affected.

II. The Level of Survivors' Benefit

515. The level of the survivors' benefit generally amounts to 70% of the minimum wage; if s/he has a child is under 18 it is 90%. The survivors' benefit of the so-called pseudo-survivors referred to in Article 4 of the Act (*see* paragraph 505) does not exceed the alimony the deceased insured person owed his former spouse (Article 17). The survivor's income will be deducted from the survivors' benefit. These are earnings from and in connection with work and not income from capital. Income from a private survivors' pension does not come under the income concept of the Anw either. Earnings in connection with work are deducted from the benefit for the full 100%. As far as earnings from work (wages and profits) are concerned, an amount of 50% of the minimum wage is left outside of consideration, as well as a third of the remainder (Article 18). Under the terms of the Anw, the concept of 'earnings from work' includes among other things (early) old-age pensions and early retirement benefits.

516. Regulations have been developed on the basis of Article 20 which are intended to prevent full overlapping of a survivors' benefit and a survivors' benefit on account of the social security legislation of another country. The payment of survivors' benefit (semi-orphan's and orphan's benefit) is suspended if this benefit has been granted to a foreigner who does not legitimately stay in the Netherlands. As soon as it has been proven that the person in question does, in fact, live or reside outside the Netherlands, payment will be resumed at his request. Exceptions to this rule may be made by general legislative measure.

§3. Orphan's Benefit

I. Conditions

517. A child who is orphaned as a result of an insured person's death is entitled to orphan's benefit as long as it has not yet reached the age of 16 (Article 26(1)). As far as implementation of the survivors' insurance is concerned, an illegitimate child whose mother has died and who has not been recognized by the father is also considered to be orphaned. This also applies if the surviving parent no longer has parental authority because he/she has been divested of it.

518. Three categories of children who are older than 16 are assimilated with a child under 16 (Article 26, paragraph 2). These are, first of all, children under the age of 21 who are engaged, not as externally living students, in daytime education or training during an average of 213 clock hours per quarter of a year. The second category is made up of children under the age of 18 who are incapacitated to work for more than 45%. The third category consists of unmarried children under the age of 21 whose time available for doing work is largely taken up by taking care of the household in which there is at least one child that is entitled to orphan's benefit.

519. The entitlement to orphan's benefit is excluded if the insured person has died within a year after the insurance became effective and if this was to be expected in view of the person's health at the time the insurance started. The entitlement is furthermore excluded if the orphan is the perpetrator of or the accomplice in the murder of the insured person (Article 27). Entitlement to orphan's benefit is also excluded for orphans who are living outside the Netherlands.

520. The entitlement to orphan's benefit ends as soon as the child no longer satisfies the conditions for obtaining orphan's benefit, and it is revived as soon as it once again satisfies these conditions. In this respect, Article 28(3), which provides when a child is no longer considered an orphan, is important. This is the case when the child is recognized as the child of the insured person or when it is adopted.

II. The Level of the Orphan's Benefit

521. The orphan's benefit amounts to a percentage of the survivors' benefit (paragraph 513). This percentage depends on the child's age on the first day of the month. If the child is younger than 10, the percentage is 32. If the child's age is between 10 and 16, the percentage is 48 and if the child is older than 16, the percentage is 64. The orphan's benefit is not income related. For suspension of payment of the orphan's benefit if the entitled person does not legitimately stay in the Netherlands, *see* paragraph 515.

§4. Obligations

522. The Anw imposes several obligations on the survivor, the orphan and his legal representative. These obligations may be subdivided in accordance with the sanctions attached to their violation. In the first place, there is the general obligation of notification. Violation of this obligation is punishable by an administrative fine. The penalty for violation of the other obligations to be observed by the survivor and the orphan or his legal representative is not an administrative fine but an administrative measure. This measure consists of the total or partial, temporary or permanent refusal of benefit.

I. The General Obligation to Inform the Benefit Administration

523. The survivor as well as the orphan and his legal representative are obliged to notify the SVB at its request or forthwith at their own initiative of all facts and circumstances which could obviously affect the entitlement to benefit, the level of the benefit or the benefit amount paid (Article 35).

524. The penalty for violation of the general obligation of notification is a fine. The regulation of the fine in Article 39 of the Act shows, among other things, that the SVB is obliged to impose a fine. Only in case of urgent reasons may the bank decide not to impose a fine. The maximum fine is EUR 2,269. It is in line with the seriousness of the conduct, the degree of culpability of the survivor, the orphan or his legal representative, and his current circumstances. Further regulations have been laid down with regard to the way of imposing the fine and its level.

II. Obligations Enforced by Measures

525. Sometimes a medical examination is required to establish whether the survivor or the orphan satisfy the conditions for qualifying for a benefit. For example, entitlement to survivors' benefit or orphans' benefit may exist in connection with incapacity to work. The person in question should subject himself to a medical examination at the request of the SVB (Article 37).

526. Verification regulations have been developed on the basis of Article 36 of the Act. These regulations are highly similar to the verification regulations of the AOW (paragraph 491). They deal with, among other things: timely communication of changes in address and social-fiscal number; due submission of information which is relevant to the benefit; submission of pieces of evidence; granting inspection of books, documents and other information carriers; submission of valid proof of identification and *attestatio de vita* of entitled persons or children abroad; obeying a summons to appear, supplying the information required and making verification possible.

527. In accordance with Article 38, the SVB must impose a measure if the survivor, the orphan or his legal representative have not (properly) observed the above-mentioned obligations. This measure is imposed in the form of a sanction by total or partial, temporary or permanent refusal of benefit. Only in case of urgent reasons may the bank decide not to impose a measure. This may be the case if the same conduct is punishable by a fine. Regulations have been laid down on the severity of the measures to be imposed.

§5. Recovery of Costs

528. The regulation with regard to the recovery of costs incurred by virtue of the Anw is similar to the one in the ZW. These costs may be recovered from the person who has caused the insured person's death and who therefore is obliged under civil law to compensate that person's survivor and orphans (paragraph 265).

Part IX. Provisions for Support in Daily Life

529. Municipalities have the task to promote support to individuals, so that they can participate in society and that they can take care of their own daily life. Thus persons with a disability (including elderly persons) or persons with psychical problems are supported to live outside institutions.

530. This obligation and further conditions are found in the WMO, that was adopted in 2015. This Act is administered by the municipalities.

531. The WMO covers the following areas:

- promoting of social cohesion, care for family members and relatives/friends who need help, and security in the municipality;
- preventing and combatting of domestic violence);
- supporting that persons with a disability or with social and psychical problems can, as far as possible in their own home, can perform their daily activities and participate in society (self-supporting);
- providing shelter for those who need this.

532. Municipalities have to make plans for their policies in these areas and the way they are to elaborate this. In making this organizations working in these areas and the citizens living in the municipality have to be consulted (in a so-called WMO council). The actual rules are laid down in a WMO regulation of the municipality. This means that the situation can vary from municipality to municipality. The *Veneniging van Nederlandse Gemeenten* (VNG [Association of Municipalities]) has made a model regulation which municipalities can adopt, but they do not have to. In practice, the model is often used and has led to some standardization of the regulations.

533. Everyone living legally in the Netherlands can make use of provisions of the WMO if he satisfies the conditions. The conditions are found in the WMO and, for the major part, in the regulations made by municipalities.

534. The provisions provided by a municipality can be of general measures, general provisions and individual provisions.

535. General measures aim to promote social cohesion and security in a municipality; to prevent domestic violence and to support care for relatives/friends and volunteers work.

536. General provisions are to promote the self-supporting and participation of citizens and the provision of shelter. Examples are transport provisions for persons with disabilities, provisions for organizing a meaningful spending of the day and localities for lonely persons. Also support in cases of domestic violence and advice to persons who want to make use of the WMO facilities are part of the support to be given by municipalities.

537. Individual provisions take the personal circumstances of the claimant into account, including the needs, personal characteristics and his possibilities for a set of services, adjusted to the person, that support his self-support, participation or shelter. These are meant to enable the individual to keep living in his own living area as long as possible. This may require adjustments to the house and equipment that cannot be considered to be belonging to the usual expenses of citizens.

538. In case a person want to receive an individual provision he has to inform the municipality where he lives. The municipality then first investigates whether the claimant needs the provision, or whether he can take care of himself, if possible with the usual help of his social network or persons providing care in his neighbourhood or volunteers. The municipality can decide that such alternative indeed exists and can then lie this finding down in a well-motivated decision (that can be challenged in a revision procedure and before Court). Second the municipality can decide that a general provision is adequate; that has priority to an individual provision.

539. If the result of the investigation is that the person satisfies the conditions, he is informed in writing on the type of provision that is available, that it can be a provision in kind or a budget, what the conditions are for the budget and on the own contribution of the claimant. Subsequently the person can make an application.

540. The decision on the application is taken by the executive board of the municipality. It can be challenged in a revision procedure and before court. The decision provides which support is reasonably necessary to compensate the restrictions that the claimant has. This gives the municipality some room to decide what provision is given. The idea is that a comprehensive form of customized support is given that takes the reasonable wishes of the claimant into account. The term reasonable takes the situation into account before the claimant needed support: the required support must be in a reasonable relation to the old situation; in other words, the claimant does not have to come in the same or even better situation. It is also relevant whether the claimant could have foreseen or prevented a particular problem (e.g., buying a house with many stairs when he is 75, and then needs a stair lift). Given the room for discretion there is some uncertainty how the court will test a particular decision; however, if a municipality cannot show by means by research findings that a particular number of hours for cleaning a house is sufficient to get a clean house, then it will order the municipality to take a new decision.

541. The individual can ask for a budget from which he can buy the support he needs. Thus he can adjust the way support is given to his own needs. A condition is, however, that the person is capable to take the responsibilities necessary to contract the support. He must also argue why he does not want to have a provision in kind. Furthermore the support he needs has to satisfy certain quality standards, that are mentioned in the WMO and in the municipal regulation. For some provisions the regulation can provide that no budget is available, for instance since that is more expensive. The regulation also provides how the amount of the budget is to be calculated. The actual payment is done by the SVB, that can check whether the support is given in accordance with the conditions and that can also check the quality.

542. The municipal regulation can provide that an own contribution is required for a general or an individual provision. It can vary from provision to provision but cannot exceed the actual costs. In case of an individual provision the own contribution can depend on the income and capital of the applicant and partner. How the individual income and capital is to be taken into account is regulated in a general decree (AMvB), thus by a national regulation, as municipalities are not allowed to have an income policy of their own. For some of these provisions (e.g., wheel chair) persons who have the income and capital to afford these themselves, are not given support at all under the WMO.

Part X. Subsistence Income Provisions and Social Assistance

Chapter 1. Introduction

543. A major objective of social security is to give a provision in the case of a loss or lack of income. This is done in various ways. First of all, specific provisions can be granted, such as the benefits for medical care (Part III) and the expenses related to taking care of and supporting children (Part IV). Second, benefits are provided by virtue of social security Acts which are intended to replace income which is lost owing to certain factors. Examples are the benefits discussed in Parts V, VII and VIII, which totally or partially compensate for the loss of income on account of incapacity to work, unemployment, old age or death. In the third place, social security law provides benefits that supplement the (family) income that for whatever reason is insufficient to cover the cost of living expenses, to an amount which is deemed adequate. Regulations that supplement the income to an amount which is necessary to cover the minimum needs of the person in question (and his family) are also referred to under the collective term of subsistence level regulations. This part is devoted to these subsistence level regulations.

544. Most subsistence level regulations have a limited personal scope. For example, the TW – Chapter 2) only applies to those who are entitled to benefit on account of their incapacity to work or unemployment. The IOAW (Income Provisions for Older and Partially Disabled Unemployed Employees Act – Chapter 3) and the IOAZ (Income Provision for Older and Disabled Formerly Self-Employed Persons Act – Chapter 4) supplement the income of the people who are covered by these Acts (and their spouses). The *Participatiewet* (Public Assistance Act – Chapter 5) has a general personal scope and, in principle, applies to the entire population of the Netherlands.

545. An essential difference between the *Participatiewet* and the other subsistence level regulations is the extent of the income test. When assessing whether the interested party (or the family concerned) disposes of sufficient income to provide for their minimum needs, the *Participatiewet* will, in principle, take all income into account, irrespective of their source. The TW and the IOAW consider only earnings in connection with business or professional life. Even more importantly, contrary to the other subsistence level regulations, the *Participatiewet* has a test on capital: if the interested party (or the family concerned) disposes of capital which exceeds a certain extent, he (they) will not be entitled to assistance. As applying this test on capital was found unjustified in the case of some categories applying for a subsistence income, the IOAW,

IOAZ and TW were created, so that these categories do not have to rely on the *Participatiewet*.

546. Not all income supplements will be discussed in this part. We should, in this context, point out that, in addition to an income replacing benefit (old-age pension), the AOW also provides for a supplement to the old-age pension if the entitled person has a partner who has not yet reached pension age and who does not have an income of his own (or a very low income) (paragraph 483). The survivors' benefit which is granted by virtue of the Anw is a mixture between an income replacing and an income supplementing benefit. The income supplementing element of the survivors' benefit is given the form of an income deduction rule (paragraph 514).

Chapter 2. Toeslagenwet

§1. Scope

547. The TW offers certain groups of persons who are entitled to benefit on the basis of a social insurance scheme a minimum income guarantee by way of a supplement to their benefit. Only persons who are entitled to a so-called wage-compensating benefit are, in principle, entitled to a supplement. These benefits are the WW, the ZW (plus sick pay in the second year) or one of the Acts offering income protection in case of incapacity to work (WIA, WAO, WAZO, Wajong). The TW came into force in 1987. Prior to 1987, these Acts (or their predecessors) themselves offered an income guarantee at a minimum level similar to that in the TW.

§2. Conditions

548. The main condition for entitlement to a supplement is that the person entitled to benefit has a daily income that is less than the social minimum amount per day applicable to him (Article 2). If the person in question is married, the benefit administration, the Uwv, when assessing the entitlement to supplement, must not only take into account the person in question's own income, but also that of his spouse.

549. The social minimum for a married person equals the statutory minimum wage. For a single person, the social minimum is 70% of the minimum wage.

550. For the TW, married people who are permanently separated are considered as unmarried. Two persons who are officially registered as partners are considered to be married. This also applies to single persons of different or the same sex who have a permanent and joint household, except for persons who are related in the first degree. The joint household concept in the TW corresponds to that in the *Participatiewet* (paragraph 592).

551. The TW only takes into account earnings from and in connection with work in business and professional life. The 'earnings from work' include wage from employment and profit from business or independently practised profession. As a rule, for a maximum period of two years, income from work is disregarded according to the following rules: 5% of the minimum wage is disregarded plus 30 of the income exceeding this 5%. The maximum disregarded income is, in total, 15% of the minimum wage.

In addition, 'earnings in connection with work' are relevant. This concept mainly concerns all kinds of benefits with a private or public law character that are intended to compensate a loss of income. However, these earnings in connection with work do not include a lump sum benefit which is paid to an employee in relation to termination of his employment (Articles 6 and 7).

552. There are several grounds for exclusion in the TW. Not entitled to a supplement is, first of all, a person under 18 (Article 2, paragraph 4) and unmarried persons under 21 living with their parents and persons over pension age. Also excluded is the married person whose spouse was born after 31 December 1971 (Article 3). This ground for exclusion was inspired by the thought that a supplement is not necessary in this case, since all members of the younger generation are assumed to participate in employment or are at least economically independent from their spouses. This ground for exclusion does, however, not apply if a child under the age of 12 belongs to the married person's household. The third ground for exclusion concerns the person whose wage-compensating benefit is not paid on account of actions or negligence on the part of the person in question for which he may be held responsible. If the wage-compensating benefit has been partially refused, it is considered to be fully paid for the purpose of administration of the TW. In other words, the TW will, of course, not compensate for the reduced benefit, as otherwise sanctions would be without effect. There is no right to supplement during the period that the person concerned is living outside of the Netherlands or staying there for more than three months.

§3. The Level of the Supplement

553. The level of the supplement is the same as the difference between the social minimum applicable to the person in question (paragraph 547) and his income and that of this spouse (if any) (Article 8). The supplement has been set to maxima in two ways (Article 8(4)). First, the supplement must not exceed the difference between the daily wage according to which the wage-compensating benefit has been calculated and the wage-compensating benefit itself. For instance, if the income is EUR 800 and benefit EUR 560, the supplement must not be more than EUR 240.

554. Second, the supplement for a married person is not more than 30% of the statutory minimum wage; for a single person with a child the maximum is 27% of the statutory minimum wage; and 21% if the person does not have to support an underage child.

555. Payment of a supplement is suspended in case of a foreigner who does not legitimately stay in the Netherlands. Resumption of payment will take place at the request of the person concerned, only if it has been proven that he is living or staying outside the Netherlands.

The supplement is not payable abroad the Netherlands, as the TW, is a special non-contributory benefit, just like the Wajong benefit (discussed *supra*). Currently, however, as a result of the *Akdas* judgment of the Court of Justice,[35] this benefit is still exportable to Turkey, since this is required by Decision 3/80. This Decision was not changed since its adoption and for this reason its rules were not adjusted to coordination regulations 1408/71 or 883/2004.

§4. Obligations

556. A person who claims a supplement and his spouse are obliged to inform the benefit administration (Uwv) at its request or forthwith at his own initiative of all

35. Court of Justice 26 May 2011, Case 485/07.

facts and circumstances which, in all fairness, could obviously affect his entitlement to benefit, the level of the benefit, the assertion of his entitlement to benefit or the amount of the benefit paid (Article 12). If the person in question does not (properly) comply with this general obligation of notification, the Uwv will impose an administrative fine. The regulation of the fine in Articles 14(a) and the following corresponds with that in the ZW (paragraphs 283 et seq.).

557. The person who claims a supplement and his spouse are furthermore obliged to observe the regulations drawn up by the Uwv to realize an effective verification of the relevant data (Article 13). In addition, he has to immediately grant inspection of his passport or driver's license at the request of that institution. If he does not (properly) observe these regulations, a measure is imposed. This measure consists of the temporary or permanent, total or partial refusal of the benefit. The Uwv is obliged to impose a measure. Only in case of urgent reasons may it decide not to impose a measure. A measure is not imposed if the same conduct is punishable by a fine. The measure is in line with the seriousness of the conduct and the extent of culpability of the person concerned. Regulations on the severity of the measures to be imposed have been laid down (Article 14).

Chapter 3. Wet Inkomensvoorziening Oudere en Gedeeltelijk Arbeidsongeschikte Werknemers

§1. Scope

558. The IOAW was adopted in 1987. This Act guarantees a subsistence level to unemployed employees and their spouses. As follows from Article 2 of the Act, the term 'unemployed employee' covers four categories of people who are unemployed and who have not yet reached the age of 65 (Article 2).

559. The first category consists of those people who, at the time they became unemployed, were older than 50 and born before 1 January 1965 and who were entitled to WW benefit for more than three months in relation to that unemployment. This means that they have satisfied the conditions for this benefit, including the so-called four out of five conditions. Also persons who were born before 1 January 1965 and after the age of 50 became entitled to a wage-related WGA benefit on basis of the WIA and whose benefit was withdrawn since they were no longer at least 35% disabled are entitled to this benefit.

560. A person must, as a rule, have exhausted his rights to WW benefit in order to be considered as an unemployed employee for the IOAW Act. The IOAW has the same provisions for refusing benefit as the WW in case of culpable unemployment (Article 20 WW).

561. If the unemployed employee is married, the Act also takes his spouse into account for the purpose of the right to benefit and its conditions. Both the unemployed employee and his spouse are entitled to benefit. The benefit is paid to the unemployed employee and his spouse, each receiving 50%, or, at their joint request, to one of them for 100% (Article 5, paragraph 2). Here again the rules, discussed previously, on the meaning of the term 'married', are relevant. This means that married people who are permanently separated are not considered as married. Two persons who are officially registered as partners are equal to married people. This also applies to unmarried people who have a permanent and joint household (Article 3). The joint household concept has the same interpretation as in the *Participatiewet* (paragraphs 592 et seq.).

§2. Conditions

562. Unemployed employees (and their spouses) are entitled to benefit if their (joint) monthly earnings from or in connection with work in business or professional life are less than the basic amount which applies.

563. For a married unemployed employee and his spouse, the (joint) basic amount equals the minimum wage per month. If the person in question is older than 21, the basic amount is 70% of the minimum wage. For single unemployed employees who are living with persons over age lower basic amounts apply (Article 5).

564. There are a number of grounds for exclusion (Article 6). For example, the unemployed employee is not entitled to benefit if he lives abroad or if he is residing there other than on a temporary basis. The unemployed employee is not entitled to benefit either if he is a foreigner and has not been unconditionally admitted to the Netherlands, or if he has been rightly deprived of his freedom. If the unemployed employee has been excluded from the entitlement to benefit, this, naturally, means that his spouse is not entitled to benefit either.

565. If one of the circumstances mentioned under paragraph 561 applies to the unemployed employee's spouse, the spouse cannot assert his entitlement to benefit. As long as the spouse is excluded from the entitlement to benefit, the unemployed employee is not considered as married but as single as far as the Act is concerned. In such a case, he can try to claim *Participatiewet* benefit.

§3. The Level of Benefit

566. The level of the benefit is the same as the difference between the relevant basic amount (paragraph 560) and the income (for married people: the joint income) from or in connection with work in business or professional life (Article 9).

§4. Obligations

567. The IOAW imposes quite a few obligations on the unemployed employee and his spouse. In respect of the sanctions, a distinction may be made between the general obligation of informing the benefit administration and other obligations. Violation of the general obligation of giving the required information is punishable by an administrative fine. If the person concerned does not comply with any of the other obligations, a measure is imposed, but no fine. The benefit administration, i.e., the authorities of the municipality where the person in question lives, are obliged to impose a measure. Only in case of urgent reason may the municipal authorities decide not to impose a measure. A measure is not imposed if the same conduct is punishable by a fine.

568. In case of violation of some of the obligations to be enforced by measures, the law itself explicitly indicates which measure should be taken. This applies if the interested party violates the obligation in order to prevent becoming culpably unemployed, if he neglects to accept suitable work, or if he does not obtain suitable work through his own fault. In case of violation of the other obligations to be enforced by measures, the law does not clearly prescribe what measure should be taken; it only indicates that the benefit is temporarily or permanently, totally or partially refused. Further regulations have, however, been laid down by general legislative measure on the severity of the measures to be imposed.

I. The General Obligation to Give Information

569. The claimant is obliged to inform the municipal authorities at their request or forthwith at his own initiative of all facts and circumstances which could, in all fairness, obviously affect the entitlement to benefit, the assertion of the entitlement to benefit, the level and the duration of the benefit or the amount of the benefit paid (Article 13(1)). If the interested party does not (properly) observe this obligation of notification by supplying no, incorrect or incomplete information, the local authorities will impose an administrative fine. The regulation of the fine in Articles 20a and the following corresponds to that in the ZW (paragraph 283).

II. Prevention of Culpable Unemployment

570. The person concerned has to prevent becoming culpably unemployed. The term 'culpable unemployment' has the same interpretation as in the WW (paragraphs 435 et seq.). If the person concerned becomes culpably unemployed, the municipal authorities will temporarily or permanently refuse the benefit for the amount of the earnings which the person concerned could have had if he had not become culpably unemployed. (Article 20(1)(b)).

III. Accepting or Obtaining Suitable Employment

571. If the person concerned neglects to accept suitable work or does not obtain suitable work through his own fault, the municipal authorities must permanently refuse the benefit in accordance with the extent to which the person in question could have earned income by doing that work (Article 20(2)).

IV. Other Obligations Enforced by Measures

572. In addition to the obligation to accept suitable work, the IOAW also has a few other obligations aimed at employment (Articles 37). The person concerned must, for example, do everything in his power to obtain employment, register as a jobseeker with the Uwv and omit anything that might hamper employment. Moreover, he has to cooperate in an examination as to the suitability for education or training and participate in any training or education which is considered necessary. The person concerned has also to be available for reintegration provisions.

573. If a benefit is granted to spouses, the relevant obligations apply to each of them. If there are urgent reasons for this in individual cases, the municipal authorities may decide not to impose temporary exemptions from the obligations mentioned in the previous paragraph.

574. Special regulations apply to parents taking care of one or more children under the age of 5.

575. In addition, there are obligations aimed at streamlining the administrative process. The person concerned must, for instance, immediately grant inspection of his passport or driver's license. Furthermore, he must supply any information which may be of interest with regard to the benefit within the set time. In addition at the request of the municipal authorities, he should cooperate in any way which is reasonably necessary for the implementation of the Act.

576. In case of violation of the above-mentioned obligations (in paragraphs 569 et seq.), the municipal authorities have to take a measure. By way of a sanction, they have to refuse the benefit totally or partially, temporarily or permanently. As mentioned before, only in case of urgent reason may the municipal authorities decide not to impose a measure. The measure is in accordance with the seriousness of the conduct, the extent to which the person concerned is culpable and the circumstances he is in. A measure will, at any rate, not be imposed in the absence of any kind of culpability (Article 30, paragraphs 3, 4 and 5). Regulations have been laid down by general legislative measure on the severity of the measures to be imposed.

Chapter 4. Wet Inkomensvoorziening voor Oudere en gedeeltelijk Arbeidsongeschikte zelfstandigen

§1. Scope

577. The IOAZ came into force in 1987 as a result of the parliamentary discussions on the IOAW. It was deemed reasonable to offer formerly self-employed people who had been forced to terminate their activities the same subsistence level guarantee as unemployed employees, as their socio-economic position was considered to be similar.

578. The IOAZ is meant for persons who have terminated their business or profession after having reached the age of 55 (older formerly self-employed persons) and who are younger than 65. A further condition is that they had to work within their own company or profession in order to maintain themselves for at least 1,225 hours a year. As far as the latter condition is concerned, their activities had to have a certain minimum scale (as defined in the Act, Article 2(2)).

579. Similar to the income provision for unemployed employees discussed in Chapter 3, the IOAZ (Article 3) is also aimed at the formerly self-employed person's spouse or partner (paragraph 558).

§2. Conditions

580. The main condition for the entitlement to benefit is that the monthly income of the formerly self-employed person (and that of his spouse) is less than the relevant basic amount (Article 5(1)) after the business or profession has been terminated. The regulation of the basic amounts corresponds to that of the income provision of unemployed employees discussed in Chapter 3, i.e., in relation to the net statutory wage (paragraph 560).

581. The IOAZ has several additional conditions with regard to the entitlement to benefit (Article 5(2) and (3)). It is, first of all, required that the formerly self-employed person has worked ten years as self-employed, or has worked the last three years as self-employed before making the application and as an employed person in the seven years before this period. In addition, it must be likely that his earnings from or in connection with work in case of continuation of the business or profession would have been permanently less than EUR 23,872 gross per year. A third condition is that the income from work in the last three accounting years must have been less on an average than EUR 23,124 per year.

582. The IOAZ has a wider income concept relevant to the calculation of benefit than the IOAZ. Not only earnings from or in connection with work within business or professional life are considered as income. Also income from capital is included, but EUR 130,081 (2016) is disregarded and the income from the exceeding capital is assumed to be 3% per year (Article 8).

583. The regulation concerning the grounds for exclusion (Article 6) corresponds to the IOAW which we discussed in the previous chapter (paragraphs 561 et seq.).

§3. The Level of Benefit

584. The level of the benefit is the same as the difference between the relevant basic amount and the income (for married people: the joint income).

§4. Obligations

585. The IOAZ imposes a number of obligations on the formerly self-employed person and his spouse. Since the regulation of the obligations and the sanctions in case of violation is largely the same as the one pertaining to the Act dealt with in the previous chapter, a separate discussion is not necessary (paragraphs 564 et seq.).

Chapter 5. The Participatiewet

§1. Characteristics of Public Assistance

586. The *Participatiewet* is a scheme whose predecessors date back a very long time, as the *Armenwetten* (Poor Laws) of 1854 and 1912 may be considered its predecessors. The Poor Laws Acts were based on the idea that poor relief should first and foremost be the responsibility of relatives, the church or a private charity institution. Only in cases where this aid was impossible or insufficient did the government step in (the subsidiary principle).

In 1963, the ABW came into force, which abandoned the subsidiary principle. The ABW departed from the idea that providing assistance is a government task. It was the purpose of the Act to guarantee a subsistence level to each and every Dutch citizen in case normal means of supporting life were inadequate. In 1996 a new Act was introduced, also called ABW. This Act was replaced in 2004 by the *Wet werk en bijstand*, whose main characteristic is that it has to be fully paid by local communities, which receive lump sum compensation from a general fund. As a result, they are responsible for the expenses and thus encouraged to develop a policy to reduce the number of recipients. In 2015 this Act on its term was replaced by the *Participatiewet;* the name of this Act, Participation Act, was meant to emphasize that claimants have to continue to participate in society, and if this cannot be down by paid work, it can be done by voluntary work or unpaid work. This can be required by the municipalities. The *Participatiewet* includes also provisions on public assistance benefits.

587. One of the essential features of a public assistance Act, also for the *Participatiewet*, is its supplementary character. This means, first of all, that entitlement to assistance only exists if and insofar as the financial resources (income and capital) of the person in question and his family are insufficient to support themselves. The supplementary character of the Act further entails that assistance is only provided if the other social security schemes do not offer (sufficient) provisions. In other words, the Act constitutes the safety net of the social security system.

588. A second feature of the Act is that it puts the claimants' own responsibility for maintaining themselves first and foremost. This, first of all, becomes apparent from the fact that the person in question has, as a main rule, to provide for his own income. Other obligations are aimed at terminating or decreasing the need for assistance. Of particular interest in this context are the obligations intended to promote that people in need of assistance provide for themselves by working. Non-observance of these obligations may cause the temporary total or partial refusal of assistance.

589. The Act takes the household as the point of reference for the right to and the level of benefit. Assistance to spouses (officially registered partners and unmarried partners living together), including with underage children if any, and to a single parent with his underage children, if any, is provided as family assistance. In order to determine the extent of the assistance, the needs and means of the family members together are taken into account.

590. One of the characteristic features of the Act is that priority be given to the reintegration of recipients into work. The so-called activation character of the Act is very important: recipients (and those not eligible for assistance) have to be supported in getting back to the labour market. This entails, *inter alia*, the obligation to accept so-called participation places, i.e., unpaid work during a certain period as exchange for the benefit. In the order of provisions of the Act and also in the way the Act is financed, this priority is realized. Unlike the Abw, recipients must not only be available for suitable work but also for generally acceptable work. Nor is there a *general* exemption from the duty to work for some categories anymore (such as parents with children); only in individual cases is exemption possible.

Furthermore, the role of the municipalities differs from that under the Abw. Municipalities are given more freedom to administer the Act so that they can respond better to individual circumstances. They are also given a larger responsibility. From a general fund, they are given the means to pay the benefits and the means for reintegration activities. The municipalities have to pay all costs from these budgets. Thus, if the budget is insufficient, they cannot claim the deficit from the State. As a result, they are encouraged to keep the number of recipients limited, preferably by helping them back into work. If they do not use all the means from the benefits budget, they can keep the excess. The reintegration budget has to be used for reintegration; if means are not used they have to be paid back.

The *Participatiewet* now covers also categories that previously could rely on other provisions. An example is that of the young disabled, who are not permanently fully disabled. New claimants can no longer rely on the Wajong, but fall under the *Participatiewet*. Apart from financial effects, it also means that the municipality is responsible for their integration in working life.

§2. Scope

I. Who Is Entitled to Assistance?

591. The *Participatiewet* is primarily aimed at persons with Dutch nationality staying in the Netherlands. They may claim assistance in case they are destitute or are in danger of becoming so (Article 11(1)).

592. Foreigners who have a permanent permit to stay in the Netherlands can claim assistance in case of destitution in the same way as persons with Dutch nationality. Some other categories of foreigners who legitimately stay in the Netherlands may claim assistance, too. Other categories of foreigners are not entitled to assistance, not even for very urgent reasons (Article 16(1)).

II. The Concept of Married Persons

593. A major concept for determining eligibility and the level of benefit is 'married person'. As is the case with other Dutch minimum benefits, this is a broad term.

594. Married persons are, of course, those officially registered as married, and those who are registered as civil partners. Married people who are permanently separated are not considered to be married.

The term 'married' is extended to two persons living in one house and having a common household (*see* next paragraph). Relatives in the first degree (parent – child) are not treated as married. Relatives in the second degree (e.g., brothers and sister) are not treated as married if one of them needs to be nursed by the other. This is the only exception to being treated as married. So the type of relationship is not relevant at all, the only condition is of having a common household.

595. A common household is assumed if two persons have their main residence in the same house and if they take care of each other either by contributing towards the household expenses or in another way (Article 3(2)). It is often difficult for the municipality to prove that claimants are living in a common household. In order to facilitate this task, the Act lists a number of situations (Article 3(3)) in which it is assumed by law that there is a common household. The existence of a common household is assumed at any rate if the people concerned have their main residence in the same house and if:

- they have been married to each other or with respect to their entitlement to assistance have been considered as married people before;
- a child was born from their relationship or if a child of one of the partner's has been recognized by the other;
- they have mutually committed themselves to contribute to the household by virtue of a valid cohabitation contract; or
- they are considered on the basis of a registration as a joint household, corresponding in nature and intent to the joint household discussed in the first section of this paragraph.

596. By a Decree, it is determined which types of registrations are taken into account. These are, for example, registrations of permanent common households under the general old-age insurance, the statutory medical insurance schemes, the TW, several tax laws (tax on wage, income tax, succession tax) and the regulations by virtue of which individual rent subsidy is granted to tenants and study grant to students. The registration is taken into account if it exists at the time of application for assistance, if it occurs during the time that assistance is provided or has existed at any time during a period of two years prior to the application for assistance.

§3. Conditions

597. The main condition for entitlement to assistance is that the single person or the married persons are destitute or is in danger of becoming so. In order to qualify for assistance, the person in question must, to paraphrase the Act, be or be in danger of getting in such circumstances that he does not dispose of the financial means to cover the necessary cost of living expenses. The destitution condition, first of all, expresses that assistance is only intended to cover the 'necessary costs of living expenses'. Second, it expresses that assistance will not be provided if the person in question disposes of sufficient 'means' to cover these expenses. In the following sections, we shall first pay attention to the 'necessary cost of living' (section I) and 'means' (section II) concepts.

598. In respect to the destitution requirement, the distinction between general and special assistance is of interest. General assistance is provided to cover the general expenses of living. Special assistance is intended to provide for certain special expenses. For special assistance, *see* paragraph 617.

599. The Act contains several grounds for exclusion. If such a ground for exclusion occurs, the person concerned is not entitled to assistance, even if he is destitute. And, finally, there is no room for assistance either if a person may appeal to another (current) provision with regard to the costs for which he is requesting assistance. In paragraph 619, we shall deal with the grounds for exclusion. The theme of section III is the relationship of the Act with other provisions which are available for the claimant.

I. Assistance Is for the Necessary Costs of Living

600. Public assistance is intended to cover the necessary cost of living expenses. These are costs of provisions which are deemed indispensable for a single person or married persons in order to be able to achieve a decent existence in accordance with Dutch standards. The 'necessary cost of living' concept has an open character.

It allows for an interpretation which depends on the socio-economic level of society at a particular time.

This may mean that the income which was considered a decent existence some decades ago may be considered insufficient now. What is considered to be a decent existence may be deemed insufficient in the future. The 'necessary cost of living' concept thus has a variable meaning, even in the same era. It allows for a differentiation according to personal circumstances such as age, health and living conditions.

601. In respect of a number of aspects, the Act explicitly indicates that these are not seen as necessary costs of living and therefore no assistance is payable for these expenses. Examples of such excluded costs are alimony payments, fines, damages incurred or inflicted or voluntary payment of contribution within the scope of a statutory insurance scheme (Article 14). Costs related to settlement of debts may not be included in the necessary costs of living either.

602. In order to avoid extensive discussions in each individual case, the term necessary costs has been elaborated in standard amounts, for married persons, persons with a child and single persons, and in age categories (*see* paragraph 606). In individual cases, it is possible to deviate from these.

II. Not Having Sufficient Resources

603. Assistance is not provided if the single person or married persons have sufficient 'resources' to cover the necessary expenses of the cost of living. The Act defines resources as, in principle, all elements of capital and income which the persons concerned have or may reasonably have at their disposal (Article 31). For this purpose the total income of married persons is taken into account. The means of persons sharing costs is, however, not taken into account.

604. Articles 31 and 32 restrict this broad concept of resources. Not included in these resources are, *inter alia*:

- child support;
- subsidies, such as housing subsidies;
- once-only bonus for the completion of training or education contributing to reintegration, up to a maximum of EUR 2,366 per calendar year (2016);
- income from work for a maximum period of six months up to 25% of this income, with a maximum of EUR 198 a month if work contributes, in the view of the municipality, to the reintegration into work.

The term 'resources' covers both income and capital.

605. In order to be considered as 'income' the means concerned relate to a period for which assistance benefit is claimed. These means can follow from work or capital or can be particular compensations, income from rent, alimony, social security benefits and refunds of contributions and tax.

606. 'Capital' is defined by the Act as the value of property which the persons concerned have or reasonably can have at their disposal, decreased by any debts existing at the time. Means which are not considered as income and which the person concerned receives during the period for which assistance is claimed, are also included in the capital (Article 34).

607. Several disregards apply to means which could be considered capital (Article 34). There are, among other things, possessions in kind which are usual – in respect of nature and value – or necessary for the person in question. In case of a self-employed person, the capital required for practising his business or profession is disregarded. Furthermore, some capital is disregarded. The disregarded capital is EUR 5,920 for a single person and EUR 11,840 for a single parent and for married persons. Also savings acquired during the period of assistance are disregarded. Finally compensation for immaterial damage is disregarded.

608. The disregarded capital is higher when it concerns capital corresponding with the house owned and lived in by the person concerned or his family (Article 34). In this case, a sum of EUR 49,900 (2016) is completely disregarded of the value of the house (which is the market value minus the mortgage). If the value of the capital is higher, the claimant is entitled to assistance insofar as it may not be required from this person to draw the available capital from his house. If the person concerned is entitled to assistance and if it is to be expected that the sum of annual assistance will exceed a certain threshold amount, assistance must be provided in the form of a loan under surety of a mortgage (if the capital in the house (value of the house minus existing mortgage) exceeds the disregarded sum mentioned above).

III. The Safety Net Condition

609. Within the system of subsistence provisions, the Act is the final provision. This entails that assistance is only granted if and insofar as other subsistence provisions cannot (sufficiently) be relied on.

610. The safety net character of the Act is described in more detail in Article 15. This Article reads that there is no entitlement to assistance insofar as an appeal can be made to a provision which, in view of its nature and purpose, is considered adequate and appropriate for the person concerned. In addition, it is provided that the entitlement to assistance does not include costs which are not considered necessary in those other provisions. For instance, if a person claims health care treatment, he has to rely on the Zvw. If this does not cover a particular treatment, the Act cannot be relied on instead. By means of this provision, the legislator intended to prevent the deliberate choice not to include certain subsistence costs in the provision at hand being evaded by granting assistance. The municipality, nevertheless, has the power to grant assistance in such a case if and as long as there are very urgent reasons. This may be the case in situations where an appeal has been made to a provision at hand, but it cannot wait for the decision of the benefit administration. However, even in very urgent cases, the municipal authorities are not authorized to grant assistance for costs related to medical treatment involving new medical techniques.

§4. The Level of Assistance

I. General Assistance

611. The recipient of assistance does not have to reimburse the assistance, not even if he becomes more prosperous later. A person qualifies for assistance if he has no capital and his income is less than the assistance standard. On the basis of the law, loans can be awarded also, i.e., as work capital for self-employed persons.

612. The Act mentions statutory assistance rates. In some cases, the specific individual circumstances may cause the municipal authorities to grant assistance at a level which is lower than the applicable statutory rate.

613. Even though the Act takes the individual situation into account, the rates are standardized in the Act, in order to ensure equal treatment of equal cases and also since this is much easier for the benefit administration. The national assistance rate for married persons (in the broad sense) of over 21 and below pension age is EUR 1,389 (2016) a month, for single parents and for single persons it is EUR 972 a month (there is no longer a difference; the extra costs for single parents are now compensated by family benefits). These are the net amounts of the statutory minimum wage; in this way a standard was fixed for the concept of subsistence income. Persons over 65 receive a higher amount; this is relevant to those who are not entitled to a full AOW benefit, since they have not been insured for fifty years in the Netherlands (for a single person EUR 1,092, for married persons EUR 1,492 together).

614. For persons ages 18 through 20, the assistance standards are much lower (Article 20). These low standards do not cover all generally necessary costs of living of the young people entitled to the benefit. The standards are based on the assumption that young persons may appeal to their parents for a supplementary contribution towards their cost of living. Insofar as no appeal can be made to the parents, there is a possibility for the municipality to supplement the assistance standard with special assistance (Article 16).

615. Special rates exist for persons living in an institution.

616. The *Participatiewet* has special rates for persons sharing costs with each other. These are persons who are sharing a house with one or more persons of age. The rate for two persons is 40% of the married persons' rate for each person. For the third person the rate is i 30% only. The sum of these amounts is distributed over the number of inhabitants of the house. For the application of this rule note a common household is required, it is presumed that the persons living in the house have advantages as they are able to share costs. Students are excluded from being taken into account for this rate. Therefore they can live with their parents without affecting their benefit. Also for persons with a commercial rent contract, the rule does not apply.

II. Special Assistance

617. Special assistance can be paid for special expenses that cannot be paid from the general assistance, nor from the income or capital of the claimant. This benefit is also payable to persons in work and recipients of other types of benefit if costs are made necessarily and are caused by specific reasons.

III. Supplement for Long-Term Low Incomes

618. Article 36 provides that a person who has had a low income for a long time and no capital above the thresholds and no prospect of improvement of his income position can be given an individual supplement.

IV. Grounds for Exclusion

619. There are various exclusion grounds in the Act (Article 13) that include:

- the claimant is legally deprived of his freedom;
- persons who are fulfilling their military or alternative national service;

- persons who are not working owing to a strike or exclusion, insofar as their lack of means is a result of this;
- persons who have their domicile in the Netherlands, but who are staying abroad for more than four weeks; for persons over 65 this period is thirteen weeks, and this applies also for persons of over 57.5 who are exempted for seeking work;
- persons who are under 18 years of age; or
- persons who are 18 through 20 years of age and who are staying in an institution.

620. The grounds for exclusion do not have an absolute character. In case of very urgent reasons, the municipality may still grant assistance to persons who are otherwise not entitled to assistance.

§5. Reintegration

I. Obligations

621. As mentioned above, a main objective of the Act is to give priority to reintegration into work and the corresponding provisions are mentioned in Article 9, i.e., before the provisions on benefit.

622. Article 9 reads that a person under pension age has, from the day he makes a claim, to seek generally acceptable work and to accept this work. He has to make use of provisions offered by the municipality, including social activation, aimed at reintegration into work, and he has to cooperate with an assessment of his reintegration possibilities. In practice claimants are more and more obliged to perform certain work while remaining entitled to benefit, this is often quite simple work.

623. Assistance recipients can also be offered a so-called Participation job. This is meant for persons that cannot be placed on a real job, and now they can perform, for a maximum of two years, unpaid work in order to acquire work experience. These jobs must be additional, thus not substitute paid work on the labour market. Those who refuse to cooperate can be subject to a lower benefit.

624. Recipients of public assistance can also be required to do work that is not directly meant for reintegration, but that is of societal value. This is considered to be in return for the benefit paid. Recipients are obliged to cooperate otherwise their benefit can be reduced (Article 9(1)(c) *Participatiewet*).

625. These obligations are under criticism, since there is a tension with the right not be subject to forced labour. So far this has not been forbidden by courts; however, a court decided that it could be a problem with Article 4 ECHR if a person has to do work for a longer period that has no positive influence at all on his chances to find work on the labour market (Court Arnhem 8 October 2008, ECLI:NL:RBARN:2008:BF7284). The Central Appeals Court has now further defined the limits for being employed under the *Participatiewet* (ECLI:NL:CRVB:2010:BL1093).

626. In case of urgent reasons, the municipality can give temporary exemptions from these obligations in individual cases. Obligations to care for another person (e.g., a child under 5) can constitute such a reason insofar as the provisions the municipality can provide are insufficient to allow for these care tasks. For instance, if an adequate childcare facility can be provided, it is possible to combine the childcare tasks and seeking work; then there is no reason for an exemption.

627. In case of married persons, the obligation to seek work and to cooperate with the reintegration activities applies to both spouses.

628. In case the child is under 12, the parent is obliged to cooperate only if the municipality has investigated whether the reintegration tasks can be combined with the care obligations.

629. If the claimant shows insufficient responsibility for maintaining himself (as is the wording in the Act) or if he does not meet the obligations mentioned in the Act, such as those of the previous paragraphs, the municipality has to reduce the level of assistance in accordance with the rules of the municipal regulation. After a maximum period of three months, the decision to lower the assistance has to be reconsidered.

II. Support of Reintegration

630. The municipal authorities are responsible for the reintegration of assistance recipients into work. In addition, they are responsible for the reintegration of persons receiving Anw benefit and of persons who do not receive benefit. This is provided in Article 7. Article 10 is the mirror provision: this entitles these categories to support in accordance with the provisions of the municipal regulation, which the municipality has to make.

§6. The Obligation to Inform the Benefit Administration

631. The claimant is obliged to notify the municipal authorities at their request or forthwith at his own initiative of all facts and circumstances that, in all fairness, could obviously affect his entitlement to assistance or reintegration into work (Article 17). The municipality can withdraw the decision to award assistance if failing to give the correct information has led to awarding assistance incorrectly or at very high level. If the person concerned has not provided required information on time or completely, the municipality can suspend the right to assistance (Article 54).

§7. Reimbursement of Assistance

632. The municipality can require the assistance recipient to reimburse assistance if it has been incorrectly awarded or set at too high an amount (Article 58). Assistance granted to a family can be reclaimed from all family members.

§8. Recovery of Assistance from Third Parties

633. Recovery of the costs of assistance from third parties is subject to strict regulations.

Part XI. Claims and Adjudication Procedures

Chapter 1. Introduction

634. When developing the first social security Act, the *Ongevallenwet* (Accidents Act) of 1901, the legislator decided to create a separate judicial procedure for employers and employees who felt wronged by the benefit administration. There were several reasons for not charging the civil judge with this task. The main reason was that the new Act dealt with disputes between a citizen and a public body and therefore not between two citizens. The civil judge was not familiar with this kind of dispute.

635. Together with the *Ongevallenwet*, the Beroepswet (Appeals Act) came into force in 1903. This Act regulated the foundation and composition of a number of *Raden van Beroep* (Boards of appeal), which had to decide on disputes between the implementing body and the citizen.

636. The Centrale Raad van Beroep (Central Appeal Court) was created to decide on appeals on decisions of the *Raad van Beroep*. The Central Appeals Court was to be made up of professional judges only. The *Beroepswet* regulated the procedure for the boards of appeal and for the Central Appeal Court. The competence of these courts has been extended over the years.

637. The 1990s brought a drastic change in the system of legal protection in social security matters. An important change concerned the introduction in social insurance schemes of a standardized litigation procedure, which is the same as for other areas of administrative law. This was done by the *Algemene wet bestuursrecht* (Awb [General Act on Administrative Law]), which replaced the *Beroepswet* to a large extent. Another important change involved district courts replacing boards of appeal as the first instance in social security cases.

638. At present, there is an almost uniform litigation procedure for the entire statutory social security system, with only a few exceptions. In disputes on contributions, for example, the competent judge is the district court, and then the Court of Appeal, instead of the Central Appeals Court. The reason is that decisions on these issues are now made by the Tax Office. Also the Zvw is no longer subject to the powers of the Central Appeals Court, but to the general courts. We will concentrate on the main procedure in the subsequent paragraphs.

639. First we will discuss the primary decision process (Chapter 2), the review procedure (Chapter 3), the appeal to the district court (Chapter 4) and the appeal to the Central Appeal Court (Chapter 5). Then we will briefly look at the possibility of lodging an appeal with the *Hoge Raad* (Supreme Court – Chapter 6). Finally, we will look closely at the special regulations that apply to (the legal protection from) decisions based on an assessment of medical data (Chapter 7). Many regulations regarding the primary decision process, the review procedure and the appeal with the regional court may be found in the Awb. This Act gives rules on decision-making and legal protection not only with regard to social security but also in other administrative law matters. As indicated by the Act's name, the Awb contains general rules pertaining to administrative law. In social security legislation, exceptions are sometimes made to these general regulations. Particular regulations on lodging an appeal with the Central Appeals Court may be found in the *Beroepswet* (Appeals Act). If in this part articles are referred to without specifying the relevant Act, these are articles from the Awb, unless clearly indicated otherwise.

Chapter 2. The Decision of the Benefit Administration

640. An important feature of social security regulations is that they clearly indicate on what grounds a person may claim a social security benefit. Also, the level of benefit to be paid is precisely described in these regulations.

641. In order to be entitled to benefit, the claimant must in principle make a claim with the competent benefit administration. This claim leads to decision, which is not made before the benefit administration has carefully examined the claim. In the following paragraphs, we shall look at the various elements of the above-mentioned decision-making process (application, investigation, decision), and we will focus on cash benefits.

642. In addition to decisions on granting social security benefits, the administrative bodies that implement the social security regulations make numerous other decisions. These include decisions on the amount of contributions payable by the employer to the employee insurance schemes. Other examples of decisions are administrative fine or on recovering an unduly paid benefit.

§1. The Start of the Procedure: The Application

643. Upon receipt of an application, the benefit administration investigates whether the conditions for the entitlement to benefit have been satisfied. The application must contain the relevant information for the benefit administration to make such an investigation. The application has to be made in writing (Article 4:1). In most cases, applications are made by way of filling out and handing in an application form. If the application has been made to the wrong administrative body, this body has to forward the application to the competent body, and at the same time, it has to notify the applicant of this (Article 2:3).

644. The regulations concerning the time of making an application are highly diverse. Sometimes a timely application is a condition for the entitlement to benefit. This is the case for the IOAZ (paragraph 579). In other Acts, the timely submission of the application is formulated as an obligation. This is the case, for instance, for the WW (application within one week after unemployment has started).

645. If the person concerned is late in applying for a benefit, benefit may be temporarily partially refused by way of a sanction. Furthermore, various regulations attach consequences to the time of application to the actual starting date of the benefit. In most cases, it has been stipulated that the benefit cannot start until one year before the application was made. This applies, for example, to the Anw, the AOW, the WIA and Wajong. The period of time by which benefit may be granted in retroaction under the WW is shorter. The benefit in case of unemployment cannot take effect until twenty-six weeks prior to application. Benefits on account of the *Participatiewet* and IOAW are not granted over a period preceding the time of application.

646. In order to enable the benefit administration to make a proper assessment of the application, numerous obligations are imposed on the applicant. One of the main obligations is that he must notify the benefit administration at its request or forthwith at his own initiative of all facts and circumstances which could, in all fairness, obviously be of interest in view of the granting of benefit. Violation of this general obligation of notification is punishable by an administrative fine. In addition, social security regulations impose several obligations on the applicant which are aimed at streamlining the administrative process. Violation of these other obligations leads to the total or partial, temporary or permanent refusal of benefit by way of a sanction.

§2. The Investigation

647. The benefit administration has to investigate whether the data supplied by the applicant are correct and complete. If necessary, an investigation has to be made into other data which might be of interest in respect of the assessment of the application. The investigation to be carried out by the benefit administration must be done accurately and for this purpose it often asks the applicant to put forward his point of view. In order to support the investigation, a large number of persons and organizations are obliged by law to supply the benefit administration with data and information that is required for the implementation of the Act. A certain measure of protection of the person in question's private life has to be kept.

§3. The Decision

648. The investigation carried out by the benefit administration leads to a decision. This decision should be made within a certain period of time. If the decision on the granting of a benefit has not been made within the set period of time, a notice of objection may be lodged (*see* Chapter 3). The duration of the decision term is not always the same. A decision on the granting of a benefit must, as a rule, be made within thirteen weeks of receipt of the application, but shorter and longer terms exist. A decision on account of the ZW exclusively pertaining to whether or not the incapacity to work exists or continues to exist, for example, must be made within four weeks upon receipt of the application.

If the granting decision cannot be made within the set term, the benefit administration must inform the applicant of the delay and state a reasonable term within which the decision may be expected. Extension of the decision terms is also possible if information has to come from abroad.

649. The decision to grant benefit lays down the right to benefit, from which date benefit has to be paid and the level of benefit. The benefit administration does not make unconditional and definite payments before the granting decision has been made. In anticipation of the granting decision, the benefit administration may provide advances if it expects that the person concerned qualifies for benefit but if it does not yet have sufficient data to make the decision to grant benefit. Some social security regulations have an explicit regulation with regard to providing advances, e.g., the WW (Article 31).

650. In case of a periodical benefit, it is necessary to note any relevant changes of the circumstances with regard to the entitlement to benefit. Both the benefit recipient and the benefit administration have responsibilities in this. The former must inform the benefit administration of any relevant changes in the circumstances. The general obligation of notification and other obligations aimed at streamlining the administrative process are highly relevant for this purpose. The benefit administration will carry out a second investigation in order to ascertain whether the person concerned is still entitled to the benefit (to the extent to which it was granted). Information supplied by third parties may also give rise to reinvestigation.

651. This may lead to a new decision by the benefit administration involving revision or withdrawal of the granting decision, involving adjustment or termination of the payments. In anticipation of the cancellation or revision decision, the implementing body may totally or partially suspend the benefit if it suspects that the person concerned no longer qualifies for a benefit (to the extent granted) but does not yet have sufficient data to decide on cancellation or revision.

652. Decisions of the benefit administration do not become effective until they have been communicated. Communication takes place by forwarding it or handing it over to the person concerned. The decision must be properly motivated and state by whom, within what period of time and with what body a review can be requested (Articles 3:40, 3:41 and 3:45).

Chapter 3. The Review Procedure

653. Before the person concerned can appeal on a decision to a court, he must first follow a review procedure before the benefit administration itself (Article 7:1). The benefit administration is obliged to hear the person who applied for review, to reassess the decision objected to and to decide within a certain period of time upon receipt of the objection.

§1. The Start of the Review Procedure

654. The review procedure is started by sending a letter to the benefit administration that made the decision (Article 6:4). The letter must be dated and signed and furthermore must contain the applicant's name and address, specify the decision and the objections against it (Article 6:5). If the letter does not meet these requirements, the applicant must be given the opportunity to rectify this omission (Article 6:6). As a rule, the term for asking review is six weeks (Article 6:7). In disputes of a medical nature on the existence or continued existence of incapacity to work under the ZW, the term is only two weeks. The term becomes effective as from the day after the one on which the decision has been communicated in the prescribed way.

655. The benefit administration to which the objection has been lodged must forward an acknowledgement of receipt (Article 6:14). If the objection has not been lodged with the competent body, it must be forwarded, after the date of receipt has been noted, as soon as possible to the competent body, and this must be communicated at the same time to the person concerned. The obligation also applies to administrative judges if the request for review was sent to them. If the applicant is late in submitting the request for review without very good reasons, the request for review is declared inadmissible (Article 6:15).

§2. Consideration of the Request for Review

656. The administrative body is obliged to hear the applicant who made a request for review (Article 7:2). It may only decide not to hear if the request for review clearly is inadmissible; if the objection is clearly unfounded; if the person concerned has declared that he does not want to make use of his right to be heard; or if the benefit administration completely agrees with the objection and makes a new decision in this light. Before the hearing, the benefit administration makes the relevant documents available for inspection by the applicant or, upon receipt of the notice of objection, it sends copies of these documents to him (Article 7:4).

657. In order to realize an adequate reassessment in the review procedure, the person who presides over the hearing is a person other than the one who took the disputed decision. The Awb, therefore, provides that the persons involved in making the disputed decision must neither chair the hearing nor be the only person to hear the person concerned. In addition, it is provided that in case the hearing is held by more than one person, the majority should consist of persons who were not involved in making the original decision (Article 7:5).

658. Decisions on the basis of the ZW and disability schemes (WIA and Wajong) are often decisions based on a medical or ergonomic assessment. If the medical or ergonomic aspect of the decision is objected to, a medical or ergonomic reassessment will take place. The medical and ergonomic reassessment upon objection is separated from an organizational and functional viewpoint, from the medical and ergonomic recommendations on behalf of the primary decision-making process. The benefit administration has appointed special review physicians and review ergonomists for these reassessments who, in principle, only carry out review procedures.

659. The statutory medical insurance schemes provide that a decision made in a review procedure may not be made until the *Zorginstituut* has given its advice on the case. There are several exceptions with regard to the obligation to seek advice. An exception applies, for instance, if the insured person objects to cost sharing or if the level of that contribution does not depend on a medical assessment. The same applies if the objection is clearly inadmissible or if the benefit administration has given in completely to the objections of the applicant.

§3. THE DECISION ON THE REQUEST FOR REVIEW

660. The decision in the review procedure must be made within a certain period of time upon receipt of the request. If a decision has not been made within the set term, an appeal to the district court may be lodged (*see* Chapter 4). Within the scope of social security, the decision term generally is thirteen weeks. Sometimes, this term is a little shorter.

661. If the objection is admissible, the contested decision will be reassessed on the basis of the objection. If the reassessment comes to the conclusion that the primary decision was incorrect, the benefit administration will revoke it and, insofar as is necessary, make a new decision instead (Article 7:11). The term 'reassessment' means that all aspects involved in the contested decision must be considered again. In other words, the decision-making process has to be done again in an unprejudiced way. The reassessment has to take place on the basis of the objections mentioned in the request for review; on the basis of reasons other than mentioned in the request, the benefit administration can also come to the decision that the primary decision was incorrect.

Chapter 4. Appeal to the Court of First Instance

§1. Conditions for Appeal

662. The requirements with regard to an appeal to the court are the same as for the review procedure (paragraph 648). The request has to be accompanied by a copy of the decision made in the review procedure. In respect of the possibility of rectification of omission, acknowledgement of receipt and the forwarding obligation, the same rules apply as for the review procedure. If an appeal is sent to the wrong body, e.g., an administrative body or an incompetent judge, it must be forwarded to the competent judge (Article 6:15). The term for lodging an appeal is six weeks (Article 6:7). The person lodging an appeal must pay a court fee.

§2. The Procedure

663. After the arrival of the appeal and upon receipt of the court fee, the procedure starts. At this stage of the procedure, the benefit administration forwards the documents pertaining to the case (official communications) to the regional court within four weeks. The benefit administration is obliged to submit a letter in which it gives its view on the grounds of appeal of the other party (Article 8:42).

664. The district court has extensive powers during the procedure, for instance in summoning parties. The court is authorized not only to summon parties but also to request them to supply written information and to submit documents in their possession (Articles 8:44 et seq.). Parties must comply with a summons and are furthermore obliged – except in case of urgent reasons – to supply the required oral or written information and to submit the requested documents (Article 8:27). If a party does not meet his obligations, the court may draw such conclusions as it may deem expedient (Article 8:31). This means that the applicant may be declared inadmissible or his appeal may be declared invalid. In some cases, parties may be ordered to pay the legal costs. The regulation also applies to the administrative body. The appeal may be declared well founded and as a consequence, parties may, be ordered to pay damages as well as legal costs.

665. Not only parties but other persons as well may be requested to supply information in writing and to submit documents. All administrative bodies as well as (former) employers of the (former) employee are obliged – except in case of important reasons – to comply with this request (Article 8:45). The regional court may, furthermore, summon witnesses, appoint experts to set up an examination, appoint interpreters and carry out an on-site examination (Article 8:46). In social security matters, physicians are often appointed as experts, as many cases concern medical issues on which parties disagree. The court must inform parties of the intention to have an expert carry out an examination. It may enable parties to declare their wishes as to the phrasing of the questions to be put to the expert. Parties are entitled to comment in writing on the examination report (Article 8:47). Parties must cooperate in the expert's examination. In addition, it is provided that a physician who has been appointed as an expert is authorized to get information on the person to be examined from doctor(s) in attendance, the insurance physician and the consultative physician of the implementing body. These other physicians must supply the information requested insofar as the person in question's private life is not harmed incommensurately (Article 8:48).

666. The examination by the court may take a great deal of time.

667. Upon conclusion of the procedure, parties are invited to appear in court. The invitation has to be sent at least three weeks before the hearing takes place. With the parties' consent the court may decide that a court examination is not required. Parties may submit further documents up to ten days prior to the court session. The court has ample powers on behalf of the court examination. It may summon a party to appear in person or by proxy (Article 8:59). It may also – in its official capacity or upon request – summon witnesses and appoint experts or interpreters (Article 8:60). Parties may also bring or summon witnesses and experts, but this is at their own expense. Before the court examination is concluded, parties are entitled to have a final say. As soon as the court examination has been concluded, the chairman will inform parties when a decision will be reached (Article 8:65).

668. Sometimes, already at an early stage in the consideration of the case, for example immediately upon receipt of the appeal or after a limited inquest, there is no reason to doubt what the court sentence should be. Continuation of the examination is not necessary if the regional court is clearly incompetent or if the appeal is evidently inadmissible, evidently invalid or evidently valid. In such cases, the court is authorized to consider the case in a simplified way (Articles 8:54 et seq.). Generally speaking, simplified consideration means that the court may conclude the examination and pass judgment without there actually being a court session. No appeal can be made against this decision, but parties can protest. The court will, first of all, assess whether the protest is admissible. If this is the case, it will investigate whether the appeal was rightly handled in a simplified way. If this has not been done rightly, it will declare the protest valid, thus cancelling the sentence protested against. The examination is subsequently continued as from the situation in which it was at the time. If the protest is declared inadmissible or invalid, the sentence protested against is maintained.

§3. The Decision

669. The court has to make its decision in the appeal procedure on the grounds of the appeal, the documents submitted and the matters discussed in the course of the examination (Article 8:69). This formula means that the objections of the person who has lodged the appeal should be the basis for the assessment of the decision. Parts of the decision which are not protested must, in principle, be left outside consideration by the judge. In other words, the judge must confine himself to the matter in dispute.

670. Lodging an appeal should not result in the applicant ending up in a worse situation: *reformatio in peius* therefore, normally is not possible. There is, however, an exception to this rule. This exception concerns decisions by the benefit administration bodies to impose an administrative fine in relation to a violation of the general obligation of notification by the person in question (e.g., paragraphs 283 et seq.). The social security Acts provide that, in appeal cases, the judge is authorized to change the amount of the fine to the detriment of the person concerned.

671. The Awb does not contain a list of grounds that the court has to apply to decide whether a decision made by the benefit administration is compatible. Instead, the administrative judge has to test the decision against legal standards. These are not only generally binding regulations and general principles of proper administration but also general principles of justice. The court must mention in writing which regulation or general principle of justice it considers violated (Article 8:77(2)).

672. The decision may determine that: (a) the court declares itself incompetent; (b) the appeal is declared inadmissible; (c) the appeal is declared unfounded; or (d) the appeal is declared well founded (Article 8:70). The appeal may be declared unfounded in spite of technicalities with regard to the decision against which the appeal was lodged, if the person concerned is evidently not harmed by this (Article 6:22).

Declaring the appeal well founded entails that the court totally or partially quashes the decision of the benefit administration. The court may also stipulate that the legal effects of the quashed decision are totally or partially maintained. In case of the appeal is declared well founded, the court may require the administrative body to make a new decision taking the court's decision into account. It may also, provided there is only one solution possible, make a new decision itself. The court may set a time for the benefit administration to make a new decision. In addition, it can impose a penalty if, or as long as, the benefit administration does not comply with a sentence (Article 8:72).

673. If the appeal is declared well founded, the court can decide, at the request of the person concerned, the benefit administration to compensate the damages incurred by the other party if there are reasons for this (Article 8:73). When answering the question if and to what extent damages incurred by a party qualify for compensation, this should be in line with civil law damages regulations as much as possible. This means that there must be culpability and a causal relationship between the activities of the benefit administration and the damages incurred. In the case law, it is decided that reversal of a decision shows the unlawfulness of the benefit administration's actions and that – with the exception of special circumstances – the culpability condition is satisfied even if the benefit administration is not to blame. In addition, there must be a causal connection between the unlawful action and the damages. If such a connection exists, there is an entitlement to compensation of the damages.[36] In the area of social security, the interest on benefits lost generally is the main element which has to be compensated.

674. The court can sentence a party to pay the costs which another party reasonably has had to incur in connection with the consideration of the appeal by the court. Also private parties can be ordered to pay the legal costs. This is possible, however, only in case of an apparently unreasonable use of procedural law (Article 8:75). Legal costs that qualify for compensation include costs of professional legal assistance provided by a third party. The amount is calculated according to a scheme based on the Awb which corresponds to the importance and the complexity of the matter and the procedural actions taken by the person providing legal aid. The

36. CRvB 30 Mar. 1995, *RSV* 1995/226.

compensation has a lump sum character. A fixed amount is paid even if the costs are much higher or much lower in reality.

§4. Preliminary Provision and Immediate Decision on the Main Issue

675. Lodging a request for review or an appeal does not suspend the effect of the decision it was lodged against (Article 6:16). This means that the benefit administration can fully maintain the effects of its decision even if the person concerned produces weighty arguments against it. The Awb (Articles 8:81 et seq.) sees to it that, in case the person concerned is harmed by the immediate implementation of the decision, he may request the court which is or may become competent in the main issue to grant a preliminary provision. A condition for admissibility is that the person concerned has asked for a review procedure or started an appeal procedure against the decision. If a request for a preliminary provision has been made and, at the same time, an appeal has been lodged with the regional court, the court's president may also, while deciding on the preliminary provision, decide on the issue of the main procedure if further examination cannot contribute towards a proper assessment of the issue. No appeal may be made against a preliminary provision sentence, but appeal is possible on the decision in the main procedure.

676. A preliminary provision may be made by the president of the regional court if 'immediate expedition requires it in view of the interests in question'. In this balancing of interests, the preliminary judgment of the president with regard to the (un)lawfulness of the decision objected against takes up an important position. The above-mentioned standards give the president a great deal of leeway. The preliminary provision may signify total or partial suspension of the protested decision. If the disputed decision concerns a rejection of an application for a social security benefit, a simple suspension of this decision will not do the person concerned any good. This is different if the president of the court decides that the administrative body has to pay (part of) the benefit amount by way of an advance. The president may allow the benefit administration to attach certain conditions to that advance.

Chapter 5. Appeal to the Central Appeals Court

677. Unless otherwise provided, an appeal may be lodged against a court decision to the Central Appeals Court within six weeks. The party who lodges the appeal has to submit the grounds for appeal and a copy of the disputed decision. Natural persons lodging an appeal must pay a court fee (benefit administrations have to pay the fee only if they lose the case).

Lodging an appeal generally results in suspension of the decision of the court of the first instance (Article 19, Appeals Act). The effect of this decision is suspended until a decision has been made with regard to that appeal.

678. The procedure for the Central Appeals Court is in accordance with the rules that also apply to appeal in the first instance. The court supervises the preparation of the case; it may gather information; may call in witnesses and experts and is in charge of the oral hearing in court. The Central Appeals Court can confirm the decision of the court, or it can quash it totally or partially and do what the court should have done (Article 24, Appeals Act). The Central Appeals Court is obliged to refer the matter back to the Court of First Instance if the court has unjustly made a declaration of incompetence or inadmissibility. The case is also referred to the court if the Central Appeals Court is of the view that the Court of First Instance must reconsider the case (Article 26, Appeals Act).

679. The possibility of applying for a preliminary provision also applies to the final appeal stage. The possibility of a preliminary provision pending appeal against a court decision is of particular interest within the scope of social security, since in most social security disputes the effect of the appeal is that the district court sentence is suspended (Article 19, Appeals Act). A claimant who won the case before the district court may request the president of the Central Appeals Court for immediate execution of the decision of the Court of First Instance by way of a preliminary provision.

Chapter 6. Reversal of Decision by the Supreme Court

680. As a rule, no further appeal is possible after the decision by the Central Appeals Court. In a limited number of cases only, an appeal may be made to the *Hoge Raad* (Supreme Court). This is the case if the dispute concerns subjects that are regulated in the same way in both social security and tax legislation. This is the case, for example, when the dispute concerns the question whether a person has been rightly or wrongly considered as being a resident under the national insurance schemes. A dispute on the term *wage* in the Wet FSV or the term *common household* in a social security Act may also be presented to the Supreme Court. The Supreme Court considers only legal questions. It therefore bases its decisions on the facts such as they have been ascertained by the lower court.

Chapter 7. Special Rules for Medical Decisions

681. In case of a decision on a disability benefit made by virtue of the WIA, the employee whom this decision concerns is not the only interested party. The employer generally also has to be considered as an interested party because the level of the contribution that he has to pay on account of the WIA depends on the amount of the disability benefits paid to persons who were employed by him at the time when their incapacity to work started for the first five years (paragraph 124). The circumstance that the employer must be considered as an interested party in case of a decision on the disability benefit of his (former) employee carries with it that this decision must not only be communicated to the employee, but also to the employer. Furthermore, the employer can participate in the procedure. In order to safeguard the employee's privacy, it was deemed necessary to incorporate a number of special regulations in the WIA for decisions based on an assessment of medical information, the so-called medical decisions.

682. A point of departure is that the employer is only entitled to inspection or knowledge of any document containing medical information with regard to the employee, or that he may expect that such a document is forwarded to him if the employee has given written permission to this effect. If the employee does not give his permission, knowledge of documents containing medical information is limited to a physician as authorized representative of the employer or a lawyer representing the employer (Article 105 WIA).

683. If the employee does not give his permission, the Uwv must state the motivation of a medical decision, insofar as it concerns the employee's medical data, in a separate appendix. This appendix is not given to the employer. However, upon request, it will be given to the representative of the employer. The same applies to a report or a recommendation by a physician or a psychologist which is referred to in the motivation of a medical decision.

684. If an objection or an appeal is lodged (by the employer, the employee or both) against a medical decision, the grounds of the objection and the appeal pertaining to medical data must be stated in a separate appendix. In addition, the employer is not allowed to be present at the examination in court, insofar as this examination pertains to the employee's medical data. As a result of case law, this rule does not apply automatically; the court has to decide in each case whether or not there are grounds to deal with the case behind closed doors.

685. Insofar as is required, the above-mentioned regulations must also be observed within the framework of a preliminary provision procedure and when the Central Appeals Court is considering an appeal.

Selected Bibliography

Adviescommissie arbeidsongeschiktheid (Commission Donner). *Werk maken van arbeidsgeschiktheid*. Den Haag: SDU, 2001.

Barentsen, B. *Arbeidsongeschiktheid: aansprakelijkheid, bescherming en compensatie*. Kluwer: Kluwer, 2003.

Beveridge, W. *Social Security and Allied Services*. Cmnd., 6404. London: HMSO, 1942.

Damsteegt, A. *De aansluiting van de werkloosheidswet op het ontslagrecht*. Den Haag: Boom, 2003.

Einerhand, M.G.K., et al. *Sickness and Invalidity Arrangements*. The Hague: VUGA, 1995.

Fluit, P.S. *Verzekeringen van solidariteit*. Deventer: Kluwer, 2002.

Jacobs, A.T.J.M. (ed.). *Het Nederlandse sociale zekerheidsrecht en de minimumnormen van de IAO en de Raad van Europa*. Deventer: Kluwer, 1992.

Jaspers, A. & L. Betten (eds). *25 Years European Social Charter*. Deventer: Kluwer, 1988.

Klosse, S. *Menselijke schade: vergoeden of herstellen? De werking van (re) integratiebepalingen voor gehandicapten in de Bondsrepubliek Duitsland en Nederland*. Antwerpen/Apeldoorn: Maklu, 1989.

Klosse, S. & G. Vonk. *Socialezekerheidsrecht*. Deventer: Kluwer, 2014.

Pennings, F. *Benefits of Doubt: A Comparative Study of the Legal Aspects of Employment and Unemployment Schemes in Great-Britain, Germany, France and the Netherlands*. Deventer: Kluwer Law International, 1990.

Pennings, F.J.L. & A. Damsteegt. *De Werkloosheidswet*. Deventer: Kluwer, 2009.

Pennings, F.J.L. *Europees socialezekerheidsrecht*. Deventer: Kluwer, 2015.

Pennings, F.J.L. *De WIA*. Deventer: Kluwer, 2010.

Pennings, F. (ed.). *Between Soft and Hard Law. The Impact of International Social Security Standards on National Social Security Law*. The Hague: Kluwer Law International, 2006.

Staatscommissie vereenvoudiging en codificatie sociale zekerheidswetgeving. *Eindrapport vereenvoudiging en codificatie van de sociale zekerheidswetgeving*. Den Haag: Staatsuitgeverij, 1982.

Westerveld, M. *Keuzes van gisteren... een blauwdruk voor morgen? Honderd jaar socialeverzekeringspensioenen in de Bondsrepubliek Duitsland, Groot-Brittannië en Nederland.* Deventer: Kluwer Law International, 1994.

Index

The numbers here refer to paragraph numbers.

Index

Index

Index

Made in the USA
Monee, IL
18 October 2026

66037578R10111